Advance Praise fo.
The Responsibilty Process

Over the last ten years I've seen time and time again how Christopher's work has created remarkable transformations in individuals, leaders, and entire companies. I've wanted a powerful next step to give people after I introduce how that transformation is possible. I'm thrilled that I can now recommend this outstanding book as a next step to unlock that potential.

—Zach Nies, investor, and VP of Education at Techstars

Traditional management was about accountability. Modern leadership is about responsibility. In his new book, The Responsibility Process, *Christopher shows you how to take responsibility in all aspects of your life. His previous book—*Teamwork Is an Individual Skill*—was one of my favorites to recommend. This one will be my favorite book gift for years to come.*

—Yves Hanoulle, Creative Collaboration Agent

I have long been a fan of The Responsibility Process. I am really happy to see this book so we can study Christopher's approach. I'm a believer in the power of small steps—taking action to make change. This wonderful guidebook will instruct that process—not just for your organization but also in your own life.

—Linda Rising, co-author of *Fearless Change* and *More Fearless Change*

Do you want the best possible life you can live? Read and integrate The Responsibility Process *into your life. You will receive benefits beyond your imagining.*

—Johanna Rothman, author of *Agile and Lean Program Management*

A game changer! This book is my go-to when I find myself feeling as though life is controlling me instead of me controlling my life. Thank you Christopher for helping so many of us find the way to live based on our personal freedom, power, and choice.

—Tami M. Cole, CEO, docstrats

Wow! The Responsibility Process *is a fabulous book. I've put so many insights into practice already. From the first pages, it pulled me in and was immediately applicable to my personal mastery and in my role as a leader of leaders.*

The five-step culture-building bridge from responsibility to accountability in chapter 9 is brilliant. It helped me diagnose organizational hotspots and see where I missed my leadership responsibility for one or more steps on the bridge. As a result, I've had more effective conversations with several of my staff. I anticipate better results for them and the organization.

—Steven Ambrose, VP and CIO, DTE Energy

I met Christopher and was introduced to The Responsibility Process in 2006. We hired Christopher to help build our manager training program, and it was a great investment in our culture and true foundation for our rapid growth based on shared leadership. The Responsibility Process is a journey to mastery, and the mental models help me catch myself. I love the formal process of taking 100% responsibility for myself and in the formation of teams, including leadership teams.

The Responsibility Process *packages Christopher's teachings in a very effective way for adoption by you or through your organization. I would recommend chapters 3–7 as a monthly book study for your team. I especially appreciated his new Catch Sooner Game and focus work required for adding clarity to intention. The language is powerful and key to wide-scale adoption with teams. I have used the Three Keys to Responsibility (chapter 4) as a structure for many talks I have given. This chapter is pure gold and anchors the book, the value, and the potential for you and beyond.*

This book represents a set of tools and structure that with a healthy mindfulness practice creates insight, integration, and empathy for others. For me this is part of lifelong practice in creating happiness, effectiveness, loving relationships, and impact. I look forward to a hard copy that I can keep close and that will replace my notes from his courses.

—Ryan Martens, serial entrepreneur; founder of Rally Software, the first Certified B-Corp to go public

The Responsibility Process is central to Catalysts' approach to leadership. It has played a significant role in Catalysts being the most popular employer in Austria 2014–2016 and the number-one IT innovator in Upper Austria. I'm excited to have this book to share with everyone interested in understanding our culture.

—Dr. Christoph Steindl, CEO and founder, Catalysts GmbH

Read this foundational, life-changing book! I leverage The Responsibility Process daily to process my reaction to events and to create consistently constructive action plans.

—Léonardo Murgel, IT executive

I highly recommend this book. I've been using The Responsibility Process for over a decade with meaningful results. In business, it provides a shared language for rapidly moving past finger-pointing and excuses toward problem resolution.

—Jamin Patrick, president and COO, RotaDyne

The Responsibility Process is a must read for anyone who seeks to unlock their ability to truly live and lead with power. Dr. Avery offers a simple and instructive guide that can easily be applied across cultures, languages, and environments. In leading a multicultural organization, I have worked to encourage teamwork, collaboration, and personal accountability as behaviors and values that support the development of our company and our service to customers. The Responsibility Process perfectly sums up what we strive to do and provides clarity and a purposeful path toward an outcome that will serve us personally and as an organization. The Responsibility Process truly is a gift and something important and worthwhile to share with others.

—Matthew M. Johnston, CEO/Directeur Général, HM.Clause

After experiencing just how transformative The Responsibility Process was to my own leadership practice, I am delighted that this book is now available. Thank you Christopher for bringing the message to an even broader audience. The lessons and tools are practical and can be applied by business leaders at any level from CEO to summer intern.

—Mary Lea McAnally, former Associate Dean for Graduate Programs, Mays Business School, Texas A&M University

THE
RESPONSIBILITY
PROCESS

The
Responsibility
Process

Unlocking Your Natural Ability to
LIVE and LEAD with POWER

Christopher Avery

FOREWORD BY HENRY KIMSEY-HOUSE
CO-FOUNDER AND LEAD DESIGNER OF CTI, CO-AUTHOR OF *CO-ACTIVE COACHING*, AND *CO-ACTIVE LEADERSHIP*

PARTNERWERKS, INCORPORATED
PFLUGERVILLE, TX

Published by
Partnerwerks, Incorporated
Pflugerville, TX

Publisher's Cataloging-in-Publication Data
Avery, Christopher.

The responsibility process : unlocking your natural ability to live and lead with power / Christopher Avery. – Pflugerville, TX : Partnerwerks, Inc., 2016.

p. ; cm.

ISBN13: 978-0-9977472-0-1

1. Responsibility. 2. Responsibility—Philosophy. I. Title.

BJ1451.A87 2016
170.9049—dc23   2016911179

FIRST EDITION

Project coordination by Jenkins Group, Inc.
www.BookPublishing.com

Cover design by Chris Rhoads
Interior design by Brooke Camfield

Printed in the United States of America
20   19   18   17   16   •   5   4   3   2   1

Dedication

Without Bill McCarley the extraordinary information in this book about how personal responsibility works in our minds would not exist. Therefore, I dedicate this book to Bill, my teacher and friend.

Contents

Foreword

Christopher Avery is examining the mental processes and strategies of personal responsibility more thoroughly than anyone else. That makes this book unique.

Other books on responsibility and leadership focus on direction. They tell you what a responsible leader should be focusing on such as engaging people and healing the planet. This book is different. Instead of espousing *what* a leader should be responsible for, it reveals *how* personal responsibility naturally works in the mind—how we take it, how we avoid it, and what we can do about it to be more effective and fulfilled. Personal responsibility is foundational to leadership. Anyone who wants to take responsibility for his or her world is going to be very curious about this book and the life-affirming information it offers.

Although, I only met Christopher recently, I am pleased to write this foreword, and I want *The Responsibility Process* to be really successful. A CEO participating in a Co-Active Leadership workshop introduced me to The Responsibility Process—the model after which this book is named. (For context, in Co-Active Leadership we define leaders as those who are responsible for their world. We look at the *being* and the *doing* of responsibility. Being is the ability to respond. Doing is the creative act. So, as a leader, I create my universe and I am responsible for what I create.) Christopher was mentoring this CEO to help build his responsibility practice—something you will start to learn to do with this book. He was so excited about Christopher's work and has such respect for Christopher that he took responsibility for making sure I was aware of The Responsibility Process. I'm glad he did.

As one of the grandfathers of the leader coaching movement, and as co-author of *Co-Active Coaching, 3rd edition* (Nicholas Brealey Publishing, 2011) and *Co-Active Leadership* (Berrett-Koehler Publishers, 2015), I'm struck by how perfectly what Christopher is doing in this book lines up with what we are doing with Co-Active Leadership. We each equate leadership with responsibility. And we are each redefining responsibility as the creative and resourceful place in our minds available to each of us—if we choose to access it. Accessing that place is leadership. By revealing the mental processes and strategies for doing that, this book amplifies and defines what a leader's job is—what a true leader is up to in the world.

What can that mean to you? Given that a leader is someone who takes responsibility for creating his or her world, it means all of us can be leaders. The most important thing is to be responsible for yourself. If you are willing to admit that you—that we all—have a dark side (where we avoid responsibility) as well as a light side (where we take responsibility), then this book will show you how to build your awareness and appreciation of both. When you take responsibility for understanding your dark side, you will be more whole as a person and as a leader, and you will know how to move to your light side and expand out into the world.

Christopher walks his talk, and I love how it shows in this book. Christopher is taking responsibility for responsibility—for revealing its secrets. It is clear that Christopher wants to understand it thoroughly so he can relate it to you and me so we will adopt it, build a responsibility practice, and share it with others.

He has done his research. In these pages, you will see that Christopher has a deep respect for clarity. He does a great job of making distinctions and explaining formidable ideas in a way that is easy for readers to get ahold of.

I also love that Christopher engages the reader by speaking directly to you. He pulls you in and through the material in a compelling way. I found myself examining my models as a husband, leader, coach, business owner, and trainer.

In reading *The Responsibility Process,* I gained a healthy respect for how easy it is mentally and emotionally to avoid taking responsibility for ourselves and our world, and how much we cope with and interact with this mental avoidance. I really like the way Christopher looks at the difference between being a generally responsible person (which most of us are) and taking 100% responsibility. By the time you finish this book, I expect you may discover great compassion and empathy for yourself and others by seeing each other not as responsible or irresponsible people, but rather as people who have the capacity to choose their world or deny themselves that choice.

It is likely as you read this book that you will immediately apply the insights and lessons to your life. One such instance that stands out for me is in Christopher's discussion of scarcity thinking. He writes so clearly about how taking responsibility aligns with abundance (in chapter 7 see the section titled "Play a Bigger Game"). As I read this section, I thought about how in our business at CTI we got lost somewhere around 2008 due to our fear response to the recession. Times were tough. Hard decisions had to be made about where to cut back and how to survive. We fell into scarcity thinking and did not realize it. For a long time we even designed it into our business from the board of directors right on out to our customers. It took us a long time to notice. Once we realized we were in a scarcity reaction my amazingly powerful partner, wife, and Queen of taking responsibility, Karen, declared that this post-recession time was a time of great opportunity and possibility and we would be well served by putting our attention in that direction. When Karen takes 100% responsibility for something watch out world because things are going to change, and indeed they did.

The Responsibility Process offers powerful coaching. Christopher doesn't just define the problem and then leave you with it the way some books do. He provides abundant tools, practices, and wisdom for taking ownership, solving problems, and developing your consciousness as a leader. I know you will enjoy this book and live a better life for having read it.

Henry Kimsey-House
co-founder and lead designer of CTI,
co-author of *Co-Active Coaching* and *Co-Active Leadership*

Preface

The inspiration and focus for this book came from three main "whys." First is what I see as the immense untapped value for every person around the discovery and application of The Responsibility Process (a little-known pattern in our minds that determines how we process thoughts about taking and avoiding *responsibility*—which is the subject of *The Responsibility Process*) to their lives. Second is my personal journey as a student, practitioner, and teacher of The Responsibility Process. And third is the thirst of those interested in The Responsibility Process.

Immense Untapped Value

So many people find The Responsibility Process foundational to living and learning; to relating; and to leading, parenting, teaching, counseling, and coaching. Because of this, I believe it deserves to be more widely known and understood. The tools presented in *The Responsibility Process* can profoundly benefit every person on the planet. It is the most important information I know regarding human learning, growth, and development, and subsequent engagement in life; personal fulfillment; and the expression and experience of freedom, choice, and power.

I am not alone in this belief. Thousands of clients, students, and others with whom I have worked attest to the foundational importance of The Responsibility Process to their life, work, and relationships. And they agree that exposure to this important material could positively change the lives of billions of people.

Personal Journey

You may wonder what qualifies me to write this book. Mine is not the perspective of yet another self-appointed moralist preaching "you should take responsibility!" No, my perspective is that of a one-foot-after-the-other practitioner, someone who is often slow to get it. In *The Responsibility Process* I share with you my substantial expertise at avoiding responsibility and my journey to taking responsibility.

How I emerged from my teens and twenties alive and never jailed, I'm not sure. I was bright and talented, however, I lacked perspective and was not interested in applying myself. I grew up in middle-class comfort. Though graced with some talent and intelligence, I graduated high school and left for college a not-very-well integrated young man. I didn't have much of a vision for being a successful and happy professional, so I didn't apply myself in college. As a consequence, I squandered the costly college education my parents had proudly saved for and offered to me. From the time I was four years old, I can remember this conversation:

"Why can't we eat at a restaurant?"

"Because we are saving for your college education. That's why."

After my subpar performance during my freshman year, my parents declined to continue paying for my tuition, room, and board. Over time, this became one of my most important life lessons about choices and consequences, and about action and inaction. I had earned the situation in which I found myself through my choices and inaction. Sometimes the only way to gain perspective is to experience the pain.

Over the next six years, I did manage to get on my feet, get back into college, handle a variety of full- and part-time jobs, earn a bachelor's degree, and start a career. I had learned how to work hard and "be successful." But

I did not know how to do so and also feel on purpose and fulfilled. I was driven by fear and anxiety of *not* being successful, instead of being inspired by the love and joy of living and pursuing a passion.

In my midtwenties, I uncovered what would be a leading question in my life: *How can I be both outwardly successful and inwardly fulfilled?* While the question confronted me with existential angst and doubt, it also eventually led me to—

- Two graduate degrees in organization science;

- Employment as a management consultant in Austin, Texas, during the technology boom of the late 1980s and 1990s, serving technical professionals at work;

- A dissertation project studying cooperation and competition among scientists, engineers, marketers, and managers in the first US technology cooperative research consortium; and,

- Cofounding Partnerwerks, my leadership and organization effectiveness firm focused on personal and shared responsibility for greater performance and fulfillment at work.

Yes, one good soul-searching question can be better than dozens of right answers. What began as an ugly caterpillar of angst morphed into the beautiful butterfly of purpose. And the pursuit provided so much inspiration and meaning that I was willing to put everything I had into it.

In 1991 the question led me to meet Bill McCarley who had begun his phenomenological study of responsibility seven years earlier. Bill's emerging model of how personal responsibility works in our minds was the most compelling model of normal psychology I had encountered. Thankfully, Bill became my mentor and I joined in his study. As of this writing, it has been a twenty-five-year applied-research project on the front lines of business leadership worldwide to understand The Responsibility Process, to practice it, and to discover reliable approaches for teaching it to others so they, too, can practice, master, and teach responsibility

The Thirst of Those Interested

From the moment I began in 1991, my study and practice of responsibility was immediately valuable and core to my team leadership skills-building business as documented in my first book *Teamwork Is an Individual Skill: Getting Your Work Done When Sharing Responsibility* (Oakland, CA: Berrett-Koehler Publishers, 2001). By about 2006 I was deeply hooked on the power of The Responsibility Process and turned my consulting business from its focus on teamwork and collaboration to a focus on leadership and responsibility. That's when the requests for this book began. People everywhere asked when I would write my book on responsibility.

Until recently I had not felt ready to begin writing. Why did I wait? Responsibility is a challenging subject. It confronts you (well, it confronts *me*). It calls for—and teaches—constant reflection and correction, intellectual curiosity, emotional growth and centering, and demonstrated results. Too many gaps remained for me between *knowing about* responsibility and actually *practicing* it. I still have gaps between what I know and what I practice, but my readiness to write this book shifted.

I'm glad to say I got over my feelings of not being ready to write *The Responsibility Process*. To those who asked, thank you for asking for what you want. This is for you and everyone you care about.

Acknowledgments

So many people contributed directly to this effort. They have my gratitude.

Most important is my wife Amy, whose love and support sustains me. Our sons John and Thom contributed in many ways, from showing me responsibility through their hearts and eyes to brainstorming ideas and reviewing stories.

I thank the Jenkins Group for ensuring that we produced a quality book: Jerrold R. Jenkins, CEO; Leah Nicholson, production manager; Yvonne Fetig Roehler, creative director; Elizabeth Chenette, editor; Chris Rhoads, cover designer; and Brooke Camfield, interior designer.

Thank you to Alan Grant, Dave Patrick, Ludmila Rotaru, and Bella Scanland who helped me envision the book and get the project started.

And a heartfelt thank you to all the friends, colleagues, members of The Leadership Gift Program, and members of two online review groups who provided stories, lessons, and chapter feedback: Joe Astolfi, Omar Bermudez, Scotty Bevill, Ian Brockbank, Gil Broza, Claude Carrier, Mike Cohn, Kimberly Coxon, Lisa Crispin, Christian Délez, Ilker Demirel, Mike Edwards, Steve Edwards, Amr Elssamadisy, Pierre Fauvel, Lloyd Glick, Daniel Greening, Yves Hanoulle, Ashley Johnson, Michael Kaufman, Robert Kirkman, Cathy Laffan, Gary Lavine, Kevin D. Martin, Yury Martynov, Kathie Michie, Denise Montana, Guy Nachimson, Oluf Nissen, Tim Ottinger, Tony Piazza, George Reed, John Robinson,

The Responsibility Process

Johanna Rothman, Harold Shinsato, Jeevan Sivasubramaniam, Jessica Soroky, Mikko Sorvari, Ari Tanninen, Joseph C. Thomas, Towo Toivola, Carrie Vanston, Dara Warde, Glenn Waters, Ruud Wijnands, and Ahmed Yehia.

I'm sure there are others I have missed. I apologize for not recognizing you here.

This book is truly a shared responsibility.

Introduction:

A More Productive Way to Live and Lead

Everywhere I turn I see good, smart, and ambitious professionals who feel trapped in lives and jobs they don't want and who think they can't change. They feel powerless. They assume *this* is as good as it gets. These are good and generally responsible people. They are *being* responsible as defined by societal standards. But that doesn't mean they are *taking* responsibility as we now know it's possible for anyone to do.

It is in your best interest to recognize that there is a difference between being responsible and taking responsibility.

You Have the Freedom and Power to Choose

During the question-and-answer session following one of my talks on The Responsibility Process, I called on a woman near the back. As she stood to ask her question, I shaded my eyes from the stage lights so that I could see her face and make eye contact. She was tall, elegantly dressed for a tech industry conference, and from her question I guessed she was either Asian born and educated or a first-generation Canadian. With a polite and penetrating tone she posed her question: "Christopher, my heritage places many obligations on us toward our parents and ancestors. Are you saying I don't have to keep those obligations?"

I knew where she was coming from. This form of question appears like clockwork after people are introduced to the difference between being a responsible person and taking 100 percent responsibility. The specific issue differs from person to person—victim of circumstance, guilt, and shame over some mistake or poor choice, feeling trapped in an unwanted situation—but the form of the question is the same: "How am I supposed to take responsibility for *this* problem?" Learning how responsibility works in our minds helps with that. It both inspires people to consider how powerful and free they can be, and it challenges them to examine their own responsibility—or lack thereof—for ongoing upsets and stuck points in their lives.

After acknowledging that her question was valid and that her life situation was worthy of self-examination, I answered her from the perspective of taking responsibility. "The way I see it" I said, "you have at least three choices, maybe more:

- You can keep the traditions and despise doing so.

- You can keep the traditions and love doing so.

- Or you can choose to not be constrained by those traditions and negotiate a new relationship with your family.

The choice is yours."

There was no way I could divine and pronounce the one "right" answer to that question that would free her from what I imagine are feelings of shame for not wanting to maintain tradition and feelings of obligation for keeping traditions she may not value. However, I can remind her and everyone listening intently for the answer: she has—and they all have—the freedom and power to choose even if they are unaware of it at the moment.

Being Responsible versus Taking Responsibility

A gulf of a difference exists between *being* a responsible person versus *taking* 100 percent responsibility. The difference, in terms of life experience and results, is vast—vast like an ocean, or perhaps a star system.

Being responsible is one of the most important tenets of every society I know. No matter where we are born, soon after we come into the world and start to make sense of our surroundings, our culture tells us at every turn to be responsible. Well-intentioned parents, aunts and uncles, grandparents, teachers, employers, the media, politicians, and those "indulge responsibly" advertisers all consistently admonish us to be responsible.

They also tell us what it means to be responsible:

- Be good.

- Do what you are told.

- Mind your teachers.

- Get a good job.

- Raise a family.

- Contribute to society.

And they tell us what it means to be irresponsible:

- Shame on you.

- Say you're sorry.

- Don't disappoint.

- Get back in line.

- Don't make a scene.

- Do it even if you don't like it.

- Wait your turn.

This is how we're molded—conditioned—through millions of daily interactions toward being responsible members of society. Being responsible means being good and acceptable in the eyes of another. It means receiving approval. It means conforming to expectations.[1]

Taking responsibility is vastly different. It means to see yourself as a powerful causal force for your experience of life. You have the ability to choose your response to situations in life. You, through your choices and action or inaction, can be seen as the primary cause for your

- happiness or unhappiness,

- success or lack of success,

- performance or lack of performance,

- limitlessness or limitation,

- engagement or disengagement,

- clarity or confusion,

- fulfillment or lack of fulfillment, and

- energy or lethargy.

Being responsible is a commitment to being good and doing right (even if you are miserable when doing so). Taking responsibility is a commitment to own your life, to self-leadership, growth, and freedom.

Though different, the two are not mutually exclusive. Indeed, I see myself as a responsible person. I imagine you see yourself that way too. However since 1991 I have identified less and less with being responsible and identified more and more with taking responsibility. A commitment to taking 100 percent responsibility will provide you with a strong sense of being responsible. But a commitment to being responsible can undermine your willingness to take responsibility at every turn. Being responsible is a commitment to feelings of safety through approval, not to feelings of freedom through self-leadership and growth. By definition, being responsible relies on feelings of shame and obligation, and in having ready-made answers of denial, blame, and justification. Indeed, consider how cultural norms for being responsible will consistently thwart otherwise good people from stepping up and taking responsibility (e.g., the good sons or daughters who follow the parents' advice to pursue a safe career as a teacher, accountant, or such, instead of thinking for themselves—then they wake up in middle age and realize they hate their career). This phenomena is rampant across societies and in company cultures.

Being responsible pales in comparison to taking responsibility. Indeed being responsible leaves many people feeling shallow or trapped, while taking 100 percent responsibility feels freeing and powerful. This book—*The Responsibility Process*—is about seeing that difference clearly through three tools, each uncovered over the past three decades, so that you can make a difference in your life and the lives of others.

Responsibility Practice

Knowing about something differs from putting it into practice. My clients and I have what we refer to as a "responsibility practice." Every day, just by living life, we are given the opportunity to practice taking 100 percent responsibility. So that you, too, can develop a responsibility practice, I offer practice sections throughout this book wherever one makes sense. This is the first.

Think of examples in your own life of *being* responsible versus *taking* 100 percent responsibility, as described in this section. What differences do you see in terms of your experience of life, work, and relationships? Which is more energizing?

The First Principle of Success

For millennia advisors have told us that taking 100 percent personal responsibility is the first principle of success. These advisors include

- philosophers such as Socrates;

- success experts like Napoleon Hill, Jack Canfield, and Tony Robbins;

- spiritual leaders such as Norman Vincent Peale and Robert Schuller; and

- management experts like Steven Covey and Marshall Goldsmith.[2]

Why is taking 100 percent responsibility the first principle of success? All your skills and abilities—your thinking tools, decision formulas, problem-solving approaches, and other frameworks—depend on your point of view about cause and effect in your life. From the viewpoint of taking 100 percent responsibility, you see yourself as agent, source, or first cause for your success or failure, happiness or sadness, results or lack thereof. Until we are willing to own it, the gurus say, we are easily stopped by problems and challenges that we perceive as insurmountable.

Popular TED presenter Derek Sivers founded CD Baby in 1998, turning it into the largest seller of independent music online with $100 million in sales for 150,000 musicians. He sold CD Baby in 2008 for $22 million, giving the proceeds to a charitable trust for music education. Speaking on his blog about his book *Anything You Want: 40 Lessons for a New Kind of Entrepreneur* Sivers confesses:

> *I cut two chapters out of my book because they were too nasty.*
>
> *They vented all the awful details about how my terrible employees staged a mutiny to try to get rid of me, and corrupted the culture of the company into a festering pool of entitlement, focused only on their benefits instead of our clients.*
>
> *Afterwards, I spent a few years still mad at those evil brats for what they did. So, like anyone feeling victimized and wronged, I needed to vent—to tell my side of the story. Or so I thought.*
>
> *So do you want to know **the real reason I cut those chapters?***
>
> *I realized it was all my fault.*
>
> *I let the culture of the company get corrupted.*
>
> *I ignored problems instead of nipping them in the bud.*
>
> *I was aloof and away instead of managing or training managers.*
>
> *I confused everyone by sharing my daily thoughts before they had cemented into decisions.*
>
> *I announced decisions, then assumed they were being done, without following-up to ensure.*

> *I whimsically delegated to the wrong people, avoiding the*
> *mental work of choosing wisely.*
> *(I could list another 20 of these, but you get the idea.)*
> *It felt so SO good to realize it was my fault!*[3]

Because words matter, I might encourage Sivers to claim "it was all my responsibility" as opposed to "it was all my fault"; however, he does it for emphasis so I'll let him slide. Why? Because the more telling phrase is "It felt SO good to realize . . ." That's important. That's why I identify with taking 100 percent responsibility. It is freeing. That's personal power! That's choice! And it comes from a point of view—a mental state of responsibility—that, as you will soon see, is available to each of us, all the time. It is the perfect mental state for solving any problem.

Sivers' blog goes on to press this point:

> *But to decide it's your fault feels amazing! Now you weren't*
> *wronged. **They were just playing their part in the situation***
> ***you created.** They're just delivering the punch-line to the joke*
> *you set up.*
>
> *What power! Now you're like a new super-hero, just dis-*
> *covering your strength. Now you're the powerful person that*
> *made things happen, made a mistake, and can learn from it.*
> *Now you're in control and there's nothing to complain about.*
>
> *This philosophy feels so good that **I've playfully decided***
> ***to apply this "EVERYTHING IS MY FAULT" rule to the rest***
> ***of my life.***
>
> *It's one of those base rules like "people mean well" that's*
> *more fun to believe, and have a few exceptions, than to not*
> *believe at all.*

The guy that stole $9000 from me? **My fault.** *I should have verified his claims.*

The love of my life that dumped me out of the blue (by email!) after 6 years? **My fault.** *I let our relationship plateau.*

Someone was rude to me today? **My fault.** *I could have lightened their mood beforehand.*

Don't like my government? **My fault.** *I could get involved and change the world.*

See what power it is?[4]

Notice Sivers' reframing from a simplistic cause-and-effect reasoning to a systems view of how he put himself in the position for each of the bad things to happen, and what he could learn to do differently now or in the future.

This systems view is what *The Responsibility Process* (this book) is about. Taking responsibility—practicing 100 percent responsibility every day—is about seeing ourselves not as right or wrong, but as an agent, chooser, problem solver, and learner in the complex interrelationships of our lives so that we can better integrate with the people and world around us. When we do this, we enjoy a better and more productive way to live and lead.

Responsibility Practice

Think of an upsetting problem (we all have plenty) for which you've mentally assigned responsibility (i.e., cause) to others or to circumstances beyond your control. Then consider how freeing (and yes, perhaps humbling too) it might be to take a different viewpoint—a point of view from which you see your possible role in setting up that problem. Don't jump to self-blame, or apply judgments of right or wrong, or good or bad. Simply see possible causes and effects of your action or inaction.

Were you successful with this application exercise?

If so, note the potential personal leadership power in reflecting on your past choices and on realizing different choices you might make in the future.

If you were not successful, it is okay. There is nothing wrong with you. Let go of this practice for now. We'll return to this idea later and you can give it another try then.

Meet The Responsibility Process

While all those experts cited earlier may tell us to take 100 percent responsibility, they don't tell us how to do so, just that we should. The Responsibility Process shows us how. From this point forward in text, The Responsibility Process refers to the process itself and *The Responsibility Process* (using italic) refers to this book.

The Responsibility Process, derived from field-research over the past thirty-one years, is a pattern that reveals how our minds process thoughts about cause and effect in our lives.

THE RESPONSIBILITY PROCESS™

•

RESPONSIBILITY

OBLIGATION

QUIT

SHAME

JUSTIFY

LAY BLAME

DENIAL

Each position in the process is a mental state characterized by its point of view. And in each mental state, the cause-and-effect logic we apply is different. You will learn much more about this in the chapters to come. Here's a short summary (working from bottom to top):

- In **Denial** we ignore the existence of something.

- In **Lay Blame** we hold others at fault for causing something.

- In **Justify** we use excuses (i.e., blame circumstances) for things being the way they are.

- In **Shame** we lay blame on ourselves (often felt as guilt).

- In **Obligation** we do what we have to instead of what we want to.

- In **Quit** we give up to avoid the pain of Shame and Obligation.

- In **Responsibility** we own our ability and power to create, choose, and attract.

These mental positions are natural. We all experience them every day.

The bottom six mental states (Denial, Lay Blame, Justify, Shame, Obligation, and Quit) are how we cope with problems that we don't yet know how to face and solve. Think of them as coping mechanisms or defense strategies. In these mental states, our problem doesn't go away, instead we learn to cope with it.

The top mental state—Responsibility—is the mental state in which we grow to overcome problems. Derek Sivers, in the story just discussed, naturally accessed the mental state of Responsibility one day (hereafter when I refer to the mental state of Responsibility I will capitalize the word). In that state he became aware of how he likely was a causal force for problems with which he had been coping for years. He enjoyed experiencing this mental state. It felt free and powerful. It connected cause-and-effect dots for him that he had not previously connected. This gave him new choices. So he started practicing responsibility as a way of life, and it was fulfilling.

You can access and practice the mental state of Responsibility too. The discussion, tools, and practice sections in *The Responsibility Process* will help you understand, try on, and practice The Responsibility Process so that you can spend less time and energy coping with life's problems and more time solving them.

Responsibility Practice

Think about how a thorough understanding of The Responsibility Process—how thoughts about taking or avoiding responsibiity work in your mind—might support you in taking, teaching, coaching, and leading from responsibility?

This Book Is for You

Do you see problems and opportunities around you that are obviously important but no one is stepping up and taking ownership for them?

Are you tired of coping with persistent problems, wishing you could instead resolve them and be free of them forever?

Would you love for the people you care about or depend on to take ownership for their lives, work, and results so they'll be more effective and dependable?

Do you sometimes feel trapped? Are you doing things out of obligation rather than desire? This obligation can show up as resentment, frustration, exhaustion, maybe even sarcasm and cynicism. You may consider quitting but don't know what you would do.

Do you hear way too much "woe is me" talk of self-pity, surprisingly even from yourself?

If you recognize yourself in these statements, you are not alone. This book is for good, smart, caring people of integrity and ambition who want to make a significant difference in the world and who believe that sanity and humanity are catalysts for ever higher performance. I meet you every day in the client organizations I support, in the presentations and workshops I give, and in the course of living my own life. I see generally responsible people molded by life into experiencing lives they don't want and don't know how to change.

In thinking about this audience of caring, smart, ambitious people, I have organized *The Responsibility Process* content around three common life roles:

1. **Self-leadership**: You want to be a catalyst in your own life to do, be, and have more of what you want;

2. **Leadership of others**: You want to inspire responsibility in others to accomplish big things together; and

3. **Developers of people and leaders**: You want to teach, coach, facilitate, and mentor others to take 100 percent responsibility for a better and more productive way to live and work.

While we can consider each of these roles separately, my most effective clients and colleagues view themselves in all three roles at once. Not only are they striving to lead themselves, but they are also participating in a variety of networks and organizations as a peer leader, collaborator, or leader of others; and they see themselves as a teacher, coach, or mentor.

While I believe this book can be useful to people of all ages and walks of life, I direct my attention to the audience I have served since 1985—working professionals. This includes the employed, the self-employed, and the un-employed looking to be employed again. If you are in this audience, you probably have a college education or higher (although not necessarily). You are male or female, likely from age twenty-five to sixty-five. And you live and work anywhere in the world.

Simply said, you want to do more, be more, and have more. Or perhaps the word *different* is better than *more*. You might have plenty (of resources or security for instance); however, you may not like the price you believe you have to pay for them. You want to live the dream. You want out of the mental and emotional rat race regardless of your position and financial circumstances. You may feel stuck in a dead-end life, relationship, job, or career and are looking for a fulfilling change. You want to experience freedom, choice, and power (i.e., when I speak of power as a benefit of practicing responsibility, I mean "the ability to do" or what some call "self-empowerment." Recall Derek Sivers' statement about realizing the mental state of Responsibility. He said, "That's power!"). You want to live wide awake and aware, on purpose, and integrated with others and the planet.

How do I know? Like me and my clients—as individuals, teams, and organizations—you likely have ongoing upsets, frustrations, anxieties, and stress. You assume you have to put up with "how it is" or risk losing everything and being worse off. I know. I meet you everywhere I go—equally in frontline teams and in board rooms. I meet you through my website and blog and everywhere I travel to speak about The Responsibility Process. I see good, smart, effective, generally responsible people who can gain so much from learning how to apply the lessons revealed by The Responsibility Process.

Responsibility Practice

Think of something in your life experience that once caused ongoing frustration or angst for you, but that you somehow completely overcame (i.e., you saw it from a different viewpoint that allowed you to let go of those negative feelings). Got it? Now, consider that this experience of morphing from frustration to power may not have been a fluke. Instead, think about it as a mental ability that you can hone and practice. What are the implications for your life, work, and relationships?

Your Takeaways

Now let's consider likely goals for each of the three audiences. I've thought about what you might want from this book and organized it to make good use of your time and attention. These goals reflect both what newcomers to The Responsibility Process want to know and understand as well as what people ask for once they are better informed. See how they resonate for you.

Self-Leadership

If you identify strongly with this category, then I imagine you work fulltime or are between jobs and looking for what's next. You feel a strong sense of loyalty and obligation to your family and friends and may want to feel that way about your employer and team at work. You likely strive for work-life balance (or integration) and seem to regularly fall short, feeling bad about shorting either family or work—usually family, or maybe yourself (or your health). You see others who have created the life, work, and relationships of their dreams and who seem to handle life with ease, and you wonder if you will ever be able to.

As you learn more about The Responsibility Process and related tools, you realize you want to do, be, or have more (and are willing to be a catalyst to make it happen) so that you can feel happy and fulfilled (in command of your choices), get more done (powerful), and feel less stressed (free). You may be interested in knowing how your mind works—how it naturally processes thoughts about avoiding and taking responsibility—so that you can understand yourself and appreciate why you feel and think the way you do.

And as you learn how personal responsibility works in your mind, you want the keys for unlocking The Responsibility Process so that you can facilitate your own and other's movement through the process to the mental state of Responsibility. You are interested in practical applications, uses, lessons, and stories about Responsibility already learned by others so that you can leverage your time and energy to grow, learn, and problem solve faster. And finally, you want first principles, tools, exercises, and other resources to call on so that you can accelerate in your mastery.

Responsibility Practice

To truly reflect who you are and what you most want as you read *The Responsibility Process*, in the previous paragraphs, consider highlighting those goals that hit home for you, deleting those that are off base, and revising the goals that are close.

Leadership of Others

If you see yourself as a formal or informal leader who invites people to share ownership with you for a change, a cause, or a purpose, then this is for you. You probably work full-time as a company employee, as a coach or consultant, or maybe as a business owner. You enjoy being a people leader and feel a strong responsibility to be a good and effective leader. But you don't always know how. Sometimes, it's just simpler to use command-and-control mode or to back off and not lead at all.

Often you think the business culture is impersonal and heavy handed. It doesn't invite or allow people to take ownership. And you want to change that. You want to be the leader that people follow voluntarily, not because they have to. You want to cast a great shadow as a leader but also want your teammates and team members to rise and shine as leaders, casting their own shadows into a community of shared leadership and responsibility.

As a people leader, you want to know how to think and act so others will step up to personal responsibility. You want to develop your own high-integrity playbook for demonstrating responsible leadership so that you can make personal choices that support you and others completely.

And as a leader you want to understand how personal responsibility affects how human beings show up and perform so that you can make decisions and lead for high engagement and performance. You want to know how you may be thwarting responsibility taking in the people you serve so that you can be aware of the effects of your choices. As a team leader, you want to know how practicing responsibility relates to teamwork, collaboration, and peer leadership so that you can be a great team builder. As a change leader, you want to know what practicing responsibility has to do with change so that you can be an effective leader of change. As a senior leader in an organization, you want to know how to build a culture of responsibility so that you can confidently lead culture-shaping initiatives to develop a healthy and thriving culture of ownership.

Responsibility Practice

As in the previous section, highlight those goals that represent you, strike through those that are off base, and rewrite others to suit you.

Additionally, consider this. Setting aside titles and roles, what is the difference between taking responsibility for a space, opportunity, or problem, and exhibiting leadership?

Developers of People

As a teacher, coach, facilitator, mentor, parent, family member, or guardian, you want to support people in ways that bring out their best. You believe personal responsibility is foundational, and you want to help others learn to take 100 percent responsibility for their life experience.

You realize that The Responsibility Process is active in everyone even if they don't yet know it—and you realize how fundamental The Responsibility Process is to learning and living. You want to hold that space of responsibility for others so they will invite you to teach, to inspire, to help them look and see with new eyes. From this perspective, you become much more than a teacher or coach. You are a mentor because you invite others to learn the adaptive skills that you have learned—to think as you think with The Responsibility Process.

As a developer of people, you want to know how to teach and mentor others in practicing personal responsibility so that they can do it and experience the benefits in all areas of their lives. You want to understand why you must demonstrate personal responsibility at a high level to effectively mentor others so that you can become an outstanding mentor. You want tips and tools for introducing The Responsibility Process and related tools so that you can teach responsibility to people who don't yet know about it. And you want to know how teaching and mentoring people in personal responsibility differs from mainstream coaching and mentoring so that you can make conscious and fulfilling choices.

Responsibility Practice

As in the previous sections, highlight those goals that represent you, cross out those that are off base, and revise others to support you.

Also, consider how frequently tactics used by well-intentioned coaches, teachers, and parents reinforce their charges in avoiding responsibility rather than taking it. Why? What would you change?

The Responsibility Process Outline

I have designed this book to be consumed in as practical a manner as possible while inviting reflection and contemplation. You can read for concepts and ideas, tools, practice, and application or—for maximum integration of The Responsibility Process into your being—for all three. You can read this book from front to back, or you can skip to the chapters that interest you.

The bulk of *The Responsibility Process* is devoted to explaining and discussing The Responsibility Process and related tools (part II) and then applying those tools to your life, work, and relationships (part III). In part I, I lay some contextual groundwork about personal responsibility in culture and society:

- Chapter 1 "**What Is Personal Responsibility?**" briefly explores the concept of personal responsibility throughout recorded history to understand how it came to be so important and, at the same time, so varied in understanding and application.

- Chapter 2 "**Responsibility ≠ Accountability**" tackles the many ways we use these two words in life and work to talk about assignments; commitments; performance plans, reviews, and systems; management; and feelings of ownership, learning, responding, and more. If we could all get on the same page here, things would be easier.

Readers who want to get right to the tools may ask why this foundation work is important. For some people it may not be. For others, without understanding this context, the basics about The Responsibility Process and about how to practice responsibility may not make sense. If the basics don't make sense, then you risk rejecting the tools as unusable.

In part II, I introduce three proven and potent tools that you can use to directly build your responsibility "muscle" as a skill set:

- Chapter 3 "**The Responsibility Process**" provides a concise description of the mental patterns we all use to process thoughts about taking or avoiding responsibility for our lives and situations.

- Chapter 4 "**The Three Keys to Responsibility**" shows you how to unlock and interact with The Responsibility Process so that you can grow rather than cope.

- Chapter 5 "**The Catch Sooner Game**" offers you a simple and proven framework you can use to change any behavior or habit naturally.

Every practical application of taking—and avoiding—responsibility can be addressed using these three tools. It is not easy, indeed the application can be significantly challenging, but it is straightforward, and the payoff is magnificent.

By themselves, the tools mean little until put in the context of life and work in pursuit of what you want. In part III, you will make distinction after distinction about studying, demonstrating, practicing, and mastering responsibility. Each of the three tools will come alive as we look at the trials and tribulations of life, work, and relationships. Organizationally, part III is guided by the three audiences to whom this book is directed (self-leadership, leading with others, developing others):

- Chapter 6 "**Lead Yourself First**" applies the tools to show you how starting with yourself is the way to experience more freedom, choice, and power in your life.

- Chapter 7 "**Sharing Responsibility, Sharing Leadership**" looks at the many ways of inviting and allowing others to step up to a shared responsibility by demonstrating it yourself.

- Chapter 8 "**Developing Responsibility in Others**" offers principles and strategies for teaching, coaching, mentoring, and even parenting to develop personal responsibility in others.

- Chapter 9 "**Leading the Organization of Choice**" written for current and aspiring senior executives, this chapter examines why taking personal responsibility can be so rare in many organizations and how changes in leadership and culture can make a significant difference.

Finally, the conclusion, "**On the Road to Mastery**," gathers together and summarizes the themes and principles that emerge throughout this book so that you can use the most important of them in your practice going forward.

Summary

In this introduction, I invited you to consider that there is a gulf of a difference between *being* responsible and *taking* responsibility. The first refers to being of good character, being a good person, and contributing to society. The second refers to seeing yourself as a causal force for every result and experience in your life. When you do, you are far more aware of your freedom, choice, and power.

The Responsibility Process

Consistently taking responsibility calls for examining the cause-and-effect forces in our world so we learn, correct, and grow. We experience our freedom to choose and the power that lies in that freedom.

The Responsibility Process, the subject of this book, shows how the mind processes thoughts about taking and avoiding responsibility and how those thoughts are reflected in our language of cause and effect. A series of mental states, it shows how we get stuck coping and defending or how we free ourselves and grow.

The Responsibility Process is written for people who want to understand how The Responsibility Process works in their mind, so that they can practice responsibility and take charge of their life, work, and relationships for a more productive way to live and lead. This book will resonate with people interested in self-leadership, leadership of others, and developing people and leaders.

Up next in chapter 1, we sample the topic of personal responsibility throughout recorded history to understand how important it is in society and culture.

Part I

Personal Responsibility in Everyday Life

1

What Is Personal Responsibility?

It's a law. The *Personal Responsibility and Work Opportunity Reconciliation Act of 1996* (PRWORA) is a US law signed by then president Bill Clinton to reform welfare. The law provided for the following:

- "Ending welfare as an entitlement program;

- Requiring recipients to begin working after two years of receiving benefits;

- Placing a lifetime limit of five years on benefits paid by federal funds;

- Aiming to encourage two-parent families and discouraging out-of-wedlock births;

- Enhancing enforcement of child support; and

- Requiring state professional and occupational licenses to be withheld from illegal immigrants."[1]

Legislators—and others—can try to get people to be responsible, according to their desired norms. However no one can make another person take responsibility. It is a choice all individuals make for themselves. That is the fascinating thing about personal responsibility. It's about the mind. It's about our perception of cause and effect and about how we perceive ourself and others.

In this chapter, and the next, we develop our understanding of the complex nature of personal responsibility before diving into the tools for practicing and mastering it. To do so, in this chapter we hop around the recorded timeline of civilization, sampling the treatment of personal responsibility from the perspectives of philosophy, religion, psychology, literature, politics, and more. Remember, this is a sampling, not an exhaustive review of the history of personal responsibility. I hope it stimulates you to consider how you think about responsibility.

When we look at responsibility throughout history, a central theme emerges—*free will* versus *determinism* and our perceptions of cause and effect. The never-ending debate around determinism and free will reveals that for each of us taking or avoiding personal responsibility is an ongoing test of what we believe about people in general and about ourselves in particular. This contrast—of powerful versus weak, free versus burdened, and having choice versus being constrained—is the issue. It is among the most important queries and debates in philosophy, psychology, religion, and politics, not to mention leadership, parenting, teaching, policing, corrections, and more.

Since the sixth century BC philosophers have debated determinism versus free will. While philosophy has the secular debate, religion debates whether God determines our lives and fate or grants us free will. Similarly in psychology, thousands of environmental and genetic forces determine so much about who we are, yet volition is among the most cherished of human capacities. In politics, we bitterly fight for sway over individual liberties and the associated responsibility for self or other. And the legislation and litigation over these rights provides never-ending battles and drama in governing chambers and courtrooms. Leaders, parents, and teachers ponder deeply whether their charges can and will think for themselves or have their thinking done for them.

Responsibility Practice

Consider your own views on free will and determinism. How aware are you of your views and how they were formed? What would be the value of examining your views on free will and determinism?

Control the Sail, Not the Wind

One of my colleagues uses a sign-off at the end of his emails—"Control the sail, not the wind"—which is a great summary for the concept of personal responsibility. Those six words raise the challenge that we don't always get to determine the many forces that affect our experiences; however, we do individually choose whether and how to navigate those forces.

History leaves us with hundreds, maybe thousands, of maxims, principles, and pithy quotes on performance, success, leadership, and happiness. Take the "control the sails, not the wind" quip. It is a shortened and more direct version of no fewer than three other quotes. Inspirational author William Arthur Ward wrote, "The pessimist complains about the wind; the optimist expects it to change; the realist adjusts the sails." Country-music singer turned breakfast sausage entrepreneur Jimmy Dean said, "I can't change the direction of the wind, but I can adjust my sails to always reach my destination." And entrepreneur, author, and motivational speaker Jim Rohn gave us this: "It is the set of the sail, not the direction of the wind that determines which way we will go."[2]

We can trace these sailing metaphors back nearly two millennia to the first century Greek-speaking Stoic philosopher Epictetus who is widely quoted as saying, "It's not what happens to you but how you react to it that matters."[3] Motivational speaker Zig Ziglar and a host of others changed Epictetus' *react* to *respond* as in "it's how you respond that matters." Many are fond of saying responsibility is the ability to respond, *response-ability*. We may not always be in charge of what happens to us, but we can always choose our response.

Responsibility Practice

Consider how much you and those around you focus on what is happening to you (i.e., the direction of the wind) as opposed to your ability to respond (i.e., setting the sails). For some fun and insight around this idea, consider changing the common greeting "How's the world treating you?" to "How are you treating the world?"

Perceptions of Cause and Effect

The concept of personal responsibility can be traced to late in the eighth century BC, more than 2,800 years ago, to Homer's *Odyssey*. In book 1, line 32, Zeus, in speaking to the other gods, says: "See now, how men lay blame upon us gods for what is after all nothing but their own folly."[4]

We can make two observations here. First, when we talk about who is responsible for something, we are usually inferring cause and effect. In this line from Homer, Zeus says men caused their own problem due to their foolish ways, but the men are blaming the gods. The second observation is that responsibility (and by inference, cause and effect) is a popular topic of conversation when things go wrong, as things apparently did for the men referenced by Zeus in *The Odyssey*. Think about it. When things are going well, we seldom ask, "Who did this to me?" But when things go wrong, big or small, our minds seek desperately to assign cause.

Psychology has a name for this: attribution. Attribution is the mental perception of cause and effect. That means we attribute a certain effect (like unhappiness at work) to a certain cause (like a surly boss). You and I make thousands of attributions every day. We could not function without doing so. That means our thinking about cause and effect shapes our life experience.

Skipping forward from ancient Greece to the early 1900s in Austria, a young scholar Fritz Heider asked himself a question: "Why do perceivers attribute the properties such as color [texture and so on] to perceived objects when those properties are mental constructs [and exist only in their minds]?"[5] This marked the beginning of attribution research in the field of psychology. What is important about this is that we humans make up attributions of cause and effect, we believe them, and we act on them, regardless of whether they are true.

In March 1920 at the age of twenty-four, Heider submitted his dissertation to the University of Graz in Austria and earned his PhD. He wrote that we don't really know that the ticking sound we hear is made by the clock or that the rose is red. Instead, Heider said our many senses are stimulated by sights, sounds, and other inputs, and then our mind makes attributions about the causes of our perceptions. Consider Heider's big idea: "Perceivers faced with sensory data thus see the perceptual object as 'out there' because they attribute the sensory data to their underlying causes in the world."[6]

Pay attention to this notion of "out there" versus "in here" (i.e., in the mind). It becomes critically important in the practice of personal responsibility as we will learn in subsequent chapters. How so? Because it locates a problem to be solved as outside of ourselves versus inside ourselves. Here's an example. Let's say you show up at work one Monday just a few weeks into your new job, and all your team members are absent. That's strange, you think, the office is completely empty except for you. This just happened to one of my clients in Finland. Looking into it, Ari discovered the company was holding a skiing holiday but nobody had told him (did you catch that attribution of blame, that the problem was "out there" in Ari's office mates?).

"They pissed me off," Ari reported. Then, looking more deeply and clearly, he realized "they" didn't piss him off. They simply went skiing as planned. They had no intent to upset him. His reaction—being pissed off—was his own. That attribution—that they did it to him—is also his own. We can debate about realistic expectations and whether someone should have invited him, or that the company holidays were listed in the orientation material that he skipped, and the skiing plans for the day were in an email he also skipped. However this debate would only further prove the point about the accuracy of attributions about office etiquette and communication. Here's the point. Ari experienced an effect, an empty office on a Monday, and his mind attributed the cause.

The most responsible people I know develop a keen awareness of their attributions. Why? They realize they can take greater ownership of life, work, and relationships by being aware of, examining, and continuously improving their own attributions of cause and effect.

Attribution research also explains biases of all sorts. In the ninety-five years since Fritz Heider gave us attribution theory, psychology scholars have uncovered more than thirty cognitive biases such as *confirmation bias* (we overvalue evidence that supports our position and undervalue evidence that refutes our position) and the *backfire effect* (where disconfirming information strengthens rather than weakens our belief in something—for example, think about how climate warming debates become more and more polarized as evidence is presented). Another bias, *fundamental attribution error,* explains how we infer a host of characteristics about another person from one observation. For instance, we see someone who is, in our opinion, poorly dressed for an occasion and we fill in the blanks about their self-discipline, values, motivation, habits, or upbringing.

To summarize, every one of us relies on our mind's ability to attribute cause and effect. Just because we believe our attributions doesn't make them true. Since responsibility is also about cause and effect, it serves us to become aware of our attributions.

Responsibility Practice

Think of a time you were positive you knew the cause for something that upset you, and later you discovered new information that changed your perspective. How did your attributions contribute to your upset?

It's How I Respond That Counts

My sister-in-law tells a story of her son, my namesake, Chris. In second grade Chris was asked by a teacher to describe himself. With an enthusiastic smile Chris answered, "Awesome." This is a story of self-perception that has been often retold in our family and enjoyed by many. It's made better by the fact that twenty-five years later Chris is well adjusted and successful. This is a story of self-efficacy.

Efficacy is the power to produce an effect. Pharmaceutical companies tout the efficacy of their patented drug to produce the desired result. In a person, efficacy is usually called competence, or the ability to produce a result. Self-efficacy is the degree to which we believe we are competent—or in my nephew Chris's case, "awesome."

American psychologist Albert Bandura says self-efficacy is the belief in yourself and your ability to perform in ways that influence events that affect your life.[7] In short, self-efficacy is the degree to which we believe we can produce the results we want. In other words, can we take personal responsibility or ownership?

The Responsibility Process

Think back to earlier in this chapter and the quotes about the wind, the sails, and desired destinations. Someone who believes in and practices personal responsibility would likely have a high degree of self-efficacy. And conversely, someone who attributes their lot in life and work to external forces would have a lower degree of self-efficacy.

What's the value of self-efficacy?

Everyone has things they want to do, habits or situations they want to change, and goals they want to accomplish. But desire and effective action aren't the same thing. Bandura's now-famous 1977 theory of self-efficacy has become one of the most researched theories in psychology. Bandura's research shows that our self-efficacy strongly affects how we approach our tasks, goals, challenges, and problems.

If you have high self-efficacy, you:

- "see challenges as opportunities to gain new mastery,"

- "engage more deeply in activities," and

- "bounce back more rapidly from setbacks."

If you have low self-efficacy, you:

- "avoid challenges,"

- "emphasize your personal failings," and

- "have little confidence in your abilities."

The good news is that self-efficacy can be developed. There are four major sources according to Bandura:

- "Mastery experiences,"

- "Social modeling,"

- "Social persuasion," and

- "Physiological and psychological responses."[8]

Let's look briefly at each.

Mastery experiences: The experience of mastering something is the most important factor determining self-efficacy. Failure experiences lower self-efficacy, and success experiences raise self-efficacy.

Social modeling: Self-efficacy can also be developed vicariously by seeing another's success. We think to ourselves, *If they can do it, I can.* This happened to my wife Amy a number of years ago when she thought she wanted to homeschool our two boys but wasn't sure if she was up to the task. Amy attended a curriculum swap meet in San Antonio where home school parents efficiently exchanged the past year's textbooks and materials for their children's courses for the texts and materials required for upcoming years. Amy came home with newfound determination to dive into home schooling. Where did the motivation come from? "Well," Amy explains, "I was completely impressed with the homeschooled kids I met there, and not nearly as impressed with some of their parents. It occurred to me that if those regular parents can produce those impressive kids, then I can't mess this up."

Social persuasion: Encouragement and discouragement affect self-efficacy. Bandura's research says that encouragement is not as effective at raising another's self-efficacy as discouragement is at lowering it. Wow! Pay attention. Positivity and productivity are related.

Physiological and psychological responses: Our moods, mental states, body aches and pains, and stress impact how much we believe in our ability to perform. Note, it is not the emotional and physical reactions themselves but our attributions about them that raise or lower our self-efficacy.

Bandura and other psychologists also write about "personal agency." That means to be an agent in your own life to make plans, put them into action, and produce outcomes. Coaches and counselors point out to people who are displaying a victim mentality that they are giving their power away when instead they could be practicing personal agency. "Take responsibility for being a survivor rather than a victim," they say. "Take ownership."

Responsibility Practice

Let's apply Bandura's four sources of self-efficacy right now. Rate yourself on each of the following questions on a scale of 1 (low) to 5 (high).

1. *Mastery experiences.* For the most meaningful things that you want to experience in life, do you plan and take achievable action steps so that you can experience mastery and thus self-efficacy?

    Low   1   2   3   4   5   High

2. *Social modeling.* Do you actively surround yourself with people who are excellent examples of who you want to be and what you want to experience?

    Low   1   2   3   4   5   High

3. *Social persuasion.* Do you actively associate with encouragers as opposed to discouragers?

    Low   1   2   3   4   5   High

4. *Physiological and psychological responses.* Do you actively manage your body and mind in ways that support you rather than undermine you?

    Low   1   2   3   4   5   High

Looking at your self-assessment of these four sources of self-efficacy, what small changes could you make to some of your life choices that could produce large results?

Know Thyself, Examine the Evidence, and Do the Right Thing

Much of our modern day understanding of personal responsibility can be traced to Socrates, the founder of moral philosophy. A citizen of Athens, Greece, from about 470 BC to 399 BC, we know Socrates through the writings of his students, Plato and Xenophon, and from Aristophanes the comic playwright. As they portray him, Socrates must surely be the first recorded responsibility master. Unfortunately, he was executed for it, and willingly so since he had a well-documented opportunity to escape imprisonment and live a lavish life (more on that later in this section). What inauspicious news this is for those of us aspiring to mastery! However, let's not jump to faulty attributions. We need not assume that mastery leads to execution. Socrates would want us to examine the evidence.

Let's take a look.

For many people, Socrates was discomforting, especially to those who professed to know something. Through his now famous Socratic method, Socrates would merely ask people how they knew an assertion they made was true. In attempting to answer, they would expose their assumptions and judgments—i.e., their attributions, as we would learn 2500 years later—which eventually led them to confess that they weren't sure at all what they knew or how they knew it. Socrates' intention was not to belittle others or show off his superior intelligence. Instead he professed to know very little himself and, instead, that he was seeking to understand what is true and how we know.

Socrates apparently was poor, dressed in a simple robe, and did not wear shoes even in cold weather. So he was likely not an imposing presence acting presumptuous and espousing moral judgment on others. He wanted us to know ourselves, and in knowing ourselves, to then do the virtuous thing—aka the right thing—by acting on our awareness of self in relation to others. "Do right" refers to the morals and ethics inherent in our social contract with others. To do the right thing is to attend to knowing ourselves and simultaneously attend to the relationships and social agreements we have constructed with others.

Today we teach one another to own our actions, tell the truth, own up to mistakes, keep our agreements, confess wrongdoing, apologize to those who were harmed, etc. All of these demonstrate Socrates' concept of "do right" which has become known as moral responsibility, or virtue.

Socrates annoyed enough people that he was eventually arrested and charged with not worshipping the state-approved gods and for corrupting the youth of Athens by encouraging them to criticize Athenian society. Representing himself and vowing to expose the truth, Socrates instead was voted guilty by a jury of 501 Athenians. Plato makes it clear that the charges were trumped up. Plato says Socrates educated rather than corrupted youth and was devoutly religious, not only worshiping the gods of the state but also following the laws of the citizenry and his social contract to accept the consequences of his actions. In his case, choosing death (by famously drinking the hemlock) was virtuous. He was not a martyr; instead he acted consistent with his beliefs and owned his punishment.

In Plato's *Crito*, Socrates' wealthy friend Crito visits Socrates who has been in prison for seven years awaiting execution. Crito offers to bribe officials and liberate Socrates from prison. Crito argues valiantly for Socrates to accept the idea of the bribe and to allow the plan to proceed. Socrates is unmoved and says:

> *My good Crito, why should we care so much for what the majority think? . . . I have had seventy years during which I could have gone away if I did not like the city and if I thought the city's agreements unjust. I did not choose to go to Sparta or to Crete, which you are always saying are well governed, nor to any other city, Greek or foreign. I have been away from*

Athens less than the lame or the blind or other handicapped people. It is clear that the city has been outstandingly more congenial to me than to other Athenians, and so have we, the laws, for what city can please without laws?[9]

Even in prison facing death and offered liberation by a friend, Socrates faced his fear, sought to see things clearly, and challenged others to virtue—to do right. Remember Derek Sivers' newfound freedom discussed in the introduction? He freed himself by accepting 100 percent responsibility for the problems in his life. And only then could he perceive clearly and take powerful and intelligent action to have what he wanted. This is a an example of Socrates' moral virtue. Knowing what is right for yourself in relation to your society creates a healthy mind, happiness, and freedom. Even if injustices happen to you, you still have your freedom.

Responsibility Practice

You can probably identify a situation where you chose to be true to yourself—morally virtuous—instead of taking the easy way out by avoiding responsibility. You can probably also identify the opposite, when you compromised your mental freedom to avoid other consequences. I call this a hard/easy paradox. We choose the harder short-term experience of taking responsibility so that we can more easily live with ourselves and experience mental freedom for the long term. Alternatively we choose the easy escape of avoiding consequences in the short term, in exchange for the longer-term hardship of living with that situation and the ongoing guilt.

Can you apply this hard/easy paradox to a current challenge in your life and find more freedom, power, and choice in the long term?

Free Will? Or Did the Devil Make Geraldine Do It?

Killer: "You bought another dress? That's the third dress this week!"

Geraldine: "I didn't want to but the devil made me do it."

"The devil made me do it" became a wildly popular catchphrase in the United States in the early 1970s thanks to Geraldine Jones, the female character conceived of and portrayed by the male comedian *Time* magazine named "TV's first black superstar." That comedian was Flip Wilson. By now you are well aware that there is a constant tension in all aspects of society between the perception of external forces on us and our uniquely human ability to respond. Not only was the devil apparently responsible for Geraldine buying a new dress but also for driving her car into the side of the church and for a host of other things. With that phrase, Flip Wilson handed society a saying perfect for us to call up to highlight our own human frailty. Now, in times of tension about who did what to whom, we could invoke "the devil made me do it" to cut the tension and provide a laugh.

Geraldine's good outcomes where Killer was concerned were always because she exercised her will, but her bad outcomes were caused by the devil. Find "the devil made me buy this dress" on Youtube and listen to how the devil followed Geraldine, snuck up behind her just as she stopped in front of the store with the dress in the window, told her how good she looked, how much she deserved the dress, how she didn't have to buy it but just try it on, and on and on.

Theologians don't agree on whether God is deterministic or whether God grants free will. If you examine the story of the Garden of Eden for answers, you find myriad interpretations of cause and effect. The basic facts are not in dispute. Eve ate the apple from the tree of knowledge after she and Adam had been instructed by God not to, and then she gave it to Adam to eat. After that, Adam's and Eve's eyes were opened to the knowledge of good and evil. They saw their nakedness, became ashamed, covered their bodies, and hid from God in the garden. These are the basic elements of the story.

However, expert interpretations vary greatly on attributions of cause and effect. Did God grant free will before Adam and Eve ate the apple, or was free will the result of the knowledge of good and evil? Did Eve act on her own free will to eat the apple, or was it because Satan, in the form of the serpent, told her to eat the apple? And why would God allow Satan in the garden knowing Satan's intentions and powers of persuasion? And did Adam eat of his own free will or because he also heard the serpent tell Eve to eat and, besides, Eve did it first and then gave it to him?

There is no lack of interpretation of cause and effect. Let's look at this from the perspectives of free will and determinism.

What is the basic idea of free will? *Free will* is the doctrine from philosophy, religion, and the sciences of individual choice and voluntary action or volition. This doctrine holds that we are free to express our will—our wants and desires. From this point of view, humans express personal choice and their actions are not simply determined by physical or divine forces.

What is the basic idea of determinism? *Determinism* is the alternative to free will from philosophy, religion, and the sciences, that all facts and events, including human choices and decisions, exemplify natural laws and have sufficient causes. Therefore, human thought and behavior is determined solely by what comes before it and not by volition.

Consider this fun story. A philosophy scholar walks into a conference on free will and determinism. The conference had organized into two discussion groups. Approaching the determinist group, its leader asked him, "Who sent you over here?" "No one," he said. "I'm here of my own free will." The leader redirected the young scholar to the free will group. As he arrived at the free will group, he was greeted by its leader and asked, "How did you decide to come over here?" "I didn't," said the scholar, "I was sent here against my will."[10]

As the story illustrates, an important part of the debate has to do with the perception of cause and effect.

The sciences such as biology and psychology make strong arguments for determinism. Your genetic makeup determines a great deal about your metabolism; personality; and risks of addiction, diabetes, high blood pressure, heart disease, cancer, and more. Environmental factors (i.e., the circumstances into which you are born) contribute too. I recently heard that 88 percent of who we are is determined by our genes and our environment. That's a compelling case for determinism. But it isn't 100 percent. An optimist can do much with twelve percentage points of freedom.

Many people argue that humans must have free will because of the subjective experience felt in deciding. Here is the famous philosopher Immanuel Kant's argument as explained by author Will Durant: "We cannot prove this freedom by theoretical reason; we prove it by feeling it directly in the crisis of moral choice. We feel this freedom as the very essence of our inner selves, of the 'pure Ego'; we feel within ourselves the spontaneous activity of a mind moulding experience and choosing goals. . . . In a way which we feel but cannot prove, each of us is free."[11]

The renowned concentration camp survivor, Austrian neurologist and psychiatrist Viktor Frankl wrote that liberty is a physical condition that can be granted or taken away, however freedom must be taken. "Forces beyond your control can take away everything you possess except one thing, your freedom to choose how you will respond to the situation. You cannot control what happens to you in life, but you can always control what you will feel and do about what happens to you."[12] This is self-leadership.

Responsibility Practice

Identify an area of your life, work, or relationships where you feel stuck or trapped and want to feel free. Note what it is so you're able to return to it. If you are open to the idea that freedom is taken and that you take it by choosing your response, then carry this application into part II, "Three Tools for Understanding and Practicing Responsibility," where we can go to work on it.

Personal Responsibility and Governance

The phrase "personal responsibility" can be traced to the Constitutional Convention in Philadelphia as framers debated a motion "that the Executive consist of a single person."[13] The convention lasted from May to September 1787 and resulted in the United States Constitution, obviously a significant historical event. Responsibility became a top issue during six weeks of the debate in June and July 1787 as the framers focused on the role, characteristics, and staffing of the executive branch. The notion of one individual with executive powers stirred strong negative connotations of a ruling king as monarch. Benjamin Franklin asked for extended debate on such an important decision as to place great power in the hands of one individual. John Rutledge of South Carolina supported a unitary executive, invoking the word responsibility. "A single man," he said, "would feel the greatest responsibility and administer the public affairs best."[14] James Madison liked the term saying: "The responsibility of all to the will of the community seemed to be generally admitted as the true basis of a well constructed government."[15]

The phrase "personal responsibility" appeared the next day, July 18, when Nathaniel Gorham suggested an individual would feel the weight of responsibility. He said, "public bodies feel no personal responsibility, and give full play to intrigue and cabal."[16] According to Riebling "The new phrase and its implications caught on quickly. In that same July 18 session, Virginia delegate Edmund Randolph urged keeping a public record of senators' votes in order to impose 'personal responsibility.'"[17] Andrew "Hamilton used the term artfully, in *Federalist* 69, to contrast the powers of president and king. The American executive would be not 'sacred and inviolable' but impeachable and removable—ruling in a 'delicate and important circumstance of personal responsibility.'"[18]

No jokes about politicians and personal responsibility, okay?

The role of personal responsibility in governance and politics is, of course, not solely a United States issue. In his 1949 book *Human Action*, Austrian economist Ludwig von Mises wrote:

> *There is no means by which anyone can evade his personal responsibility. Whoever neglects to examine to the best of his abilities all the problems involved voluntarily surrenders his birthright to a self-appointed elite of supermen. In such vital matters blind reliance upon "experts" and uncritical acceptance of popular catchwords and prejudices is tantamount to the abandonment of self-determination and to yielding to other people's domination. As conditions are today, nothing can be more important to every intelligent man than economics. His own fate and that of his progeny is at stake.*[19]

Summary

In this chapter we sampled bits of history on the subject of personal responsibility to help us understand how we think about it. There is so much more. I probably haven't even mentioned your favorite author on the subject of personal responsibility. My language references have been USA-centric although there is nothing USA-centric about personal responsibility. My intent is not complete coverage of the topic but a small sampling of how personal responsibility has evolved throughout history. What have we learned?

- It's so popular to tell others that they should take responsibility.

- We continue laying blame after 2,800 years.

- We rely on our attributions of cause and effect regardless of whether they are true or not.

- The attributions we make about our own setbacks influence our motivation to try again and to learn.

- We can develop self-efficacy.

- We can know ourselves and be true to that awareness.

- The devil made Geraldine do it.

- The reason the United States has a single head of the executive branch—the president—is rooted in the framers' reliance on personal responsibility.

In the next chapter, I continue exploring how we think and talk about responsibility in our cutlures by looking at the ambiguity and confusion around the words *accountability* and *responsibility*.

2

Responsibility ≠ Accountability

Around the world people use the words *responsibility* and *accountability* interchangeably. Every day I receive a Google alert—that's an automated email report of a search term or phrase—for the words *responsibility* and *accountability* used within the same short phrase. And every day I receive entries quoting some pundit saying, "When is someone going to take responsibility and accountability for [insert cause I care about]!?"

In this chapter, we'll continue our look at personal responsibility in everyday life by exploring the popular usage and origins of these two terms, and while I won't demand you change your language, I will suggest considering greater clarity about what you mean when you use these terms.

How We Use Responsibility and Accountability

Not only do we use *responsibility* and *accountability* interchangeably, but we also use both words to mean many things. Here is a brief list of some of the meanings. For extra fun and enlightenment, substitute each phrase in the list for the phrase *take responsibility and accountability* using this sentence: Someone should take responsibility and accountability to ensure that no one must deal with another's dirty dishes in the office kitchen. I have made the substitution in the first two examples for you:

- admit mistakes (*Someone should* admit mistakes *to ensure that no one must deal with another's dirty dishes in the office kitchen.*)

- adopt my morals (*Someone should* adopt my morals *to ensure that no one must deal with another's dirty dishes in the office kitchen.*)

- apologize

- be dependable

- be fired

- change

- do something

- face the consequences

- fix mistakes

- lead change

- make better choices

These are just a few of the many meanings of the phrase "take responsibility and accountability." You can probably think of many more. When you look at this list of the many meanings we derive from *responsibility* and *accountability*, it's no wonder we use the two words together. We must want to cover all possible meanings!

While the list of specific meanings is long, I believe they can all be categorized into two groups each with a congruent meaning. We'll explore those two groups of meanings in the next section.

Responsibility Practice

Invest a few minutes searching the Internet for the terms *responsibility* and *accountability*, plus a third keyword of interest to you, for instance *leadership* or *software quality*. So your search could be <responsibility accountability leadership> or <responsibility accountability software quality>. In each search examine how the words responsibility and accountability are used. How do the uses compare to the claims in this chapter? Keep this in mind while reading the chapter.

I *Take* Responsibility and Am *Held* Accountable

There are two significant meanings. We use both words—responsibility and accountability—for both meanings. Here are those two meanings:

- Feelings of ownership, or lack thereof, for one's experience and associated willingness and ability to take effective action;

- The act of making, keeping, and managing performance agreements and expectations.

Personally, I prefer *responsibility* for feelings of ownership. And I prefer *accountability* to refer to making, keeping, and managing agreements and expectations. Here's a fun way to remember this: If you report to a boss and you're not clear about what you will be held accountable for, then you might want to take responsibility for finding out.

Some people prefer to use these terms in the opposite way. Here's an example salvaged from the now defunct *Oz Principle Blog* that demonstrates the diverse usage for these terms: "Responsibility may be bestowed, but accountability must be taken."[1]

My usage preference for accountability and responsibility comes from the word origins, or etymology. *Accountability* means that if called on, you can give an accounting. You can tell what happened. So to hold another to account means to consider that person's story (i.e., their account) about what transpired. *Responsibility* means the ability to respond. It implies owning your power and ability to choose your response.

I see accountability as other oriented, and focused on what happened in the past. Responsibility, for me, is self-oriented, and focused on the present.

Another distinction for me is that accountability is outside of you, or at least in between you and another person. Whether you are held to account is not up to you; it comes from the people who have expectations of you. However responsibility is completely inside. Responsibility is a feeling of ownership. Hence it is subjective (i.e., different for each person). Responsibility is also transient in that it comes and goes. Sometimes I feel willing and able to respond to what's happening, and other times I don't.

Responsibility Practice

Answer the next two questions to apply these two meanings and to see if they make sense and help clarify how you use *responsibility* and *accountability*.

Do you have things in your life for which you have such great feelings of ownership that no one else ever needs to hold you to account? What are they?

Do you have things for which you get held to account by others and, truthfully speaking, that you don't really have great feelings of ownership for? What are they?

Accountability Is Imprecise

Earlier, I suggested accountability is outside or external to you. So whether or not you are held accountable isn't up to you. It's up to others. Here's a test: Have you ever been held to account for something you don't think you should have been? I thought so. Me too. And I bet there have been times you haven't been held accountable for a positive action or result of which you were proud. They did not notice, or if they did notice they did not acknowledge you. If this sounds a bit odd, then it reinforces a common belief that being held to account is only a negative experience of laying blame because it is in response to a perceived failure to meet expectations.

Systematically managing accountabilities is the purpose of any organizational hierarchy. It is a primary reason for hierarchy. You could say accountability is the first tool of management. Think about it. An organization forms because there is more work to be done than one person can do. So we hire people, divide up the work, and delegate the pieces of work across the people. This is the process of accountability, also known as delegation, and also called performance management. Most managers and companies I see could be much much better at managing accountability by taking responsibility for the imprecise and complicated nature of accountability. Does each party share clear expectations about accountability? Does each party take responsibility for generating this shared clarity? The next section considers this relationship between accountability and responsibility.

Responsibility Practice

If you are now or ever have been accountable to another, think of three times—without blaming yourself or another person—when that relationship proved that accountability is imprecise, either by thinking of a time that you were unfairly held to account, or by thinking of a time when you were proud of meeting an accountability and they did not seem to notice.

If you are in a position where you hold others to account, open a question to hold in your mind as you read this book: Accepting this imprecise nature of accountability, how then can I become a more effective leader of others?

Responsibility Always Trumps Accountability

Let me call your attention to a multitrillion-dollar problem in organizations everywhere. Positional leaders at all levels place holding others to account ahead of developing feelings of personal responsibility. As a result, work and workers suffer.

Our internal sense of responsibility, whether high or low, is a far more powerful determinant of our actions and results than is the accountability relationship. Think about it. If a person's willingness and ability to respond is poorly matched for his or her assignment (i.e., accountabilities), then the work will suffer. And, if the environment penalizes people for actually taking responsibility—for thinking for themselves, and being proactive in solving the real problem instead of doing as they are told—then even good, smart, caring people will avoid taking responsibility, and the work will suffer.

Historically management has overfocused on the accounting aspect of performance management and underfocused on people's natural willingness and ability to respond. Why? If you hold the belief that people need to be watched and measured to make sure they are performing, then performance management systems are precise-looking tools and processes a business can invest in to increase perceived control over the business. However, understanding how to craft a culture of responsibility where people naturally step up, take ownership, and perform highly— well, that's messy, imprecise, and challenging leadership work. Managing accountabilities offers a sense of certainty, even if it is false certainty. Leading from and for personal responsibility appears more complex and less certain.

Managing accountability is the systemic stuff of management. In larger systems, it is likely necessary to some degree but not sufficient. Creating a culture of responsibility is the stuff of leadership and will be addressed in chapters to come.

In the final three sections of this chapter, we'll explore how leaders and managers systematically drive personal responsibility out of people, teams, and organizations; how they could invite and attract greater personal responsibility; and how to make accountability unnecessary.

Responsibility Practice

Think of a time someone influenced you to want to step up and take personal responsibility for something.

How did it happen?

What was it that drove your desire to take responsibility?

Does this particular situation lend itself more toward a performance review system or an informal chat with those who inspired you?

Have you ever been that influential leader inspiring someone else? Think back and reflect on how that happened.

Driving Accountability Reduces Feelings of Ownership

Remember that there is a gulf of a difference between being responsible and taking 100 percent responsibility. Most accountability processes focus people on being responsible (i.e., being good and staying out of trouble) rather than taking 100 percent responsibility. The more we focus on driving accountability into the person, team, or organization, the more we thwart people from taking responsibility.

Why? Accountability is based on a credible threat ("accomplish X or face the consequences"). Thus it is perceived as a negative, not a positive, relationship process. So with it comes fear. And when fear goes up, responsibility goes down. You'll understand how this works in the next chapter as you become familiar with The Responsibility Process.

With low levels of ownership and responsibility, accountability systems often grow even more onerous and complex in an attempt to control performance. "We need greater accountability!" management says to HR. "Find a more comprehensive performance management system!" So the organization adds more layers of control and documentation, and employees become even more constrained and less able to respond effectively. Avoiding responsibility is the easy way to be safe in such a system.

The cycle continues until an enlightened senior leader sees the fallacy in the thinking about driving accountability into the organization and focuses instead on developing a culture of responsibility.

Responsibility Practice

Think of a time when an authority figure in your life did something that discouraged you or your team from taking responsibility, instead focusing on personal safety and compliance. As you become more aware of the dynamics of personal responsibility through the course of this book, consider how you allowed that to happen and what different choices you could make in the future to always retain your sense of responsibility.

Now, think of a time when you did something that discouraged one of your charges, teams, or an entire organization from stepping up to responsibility. What awareness could you develop as you read this book to choose to never do that again?

Invite and Attract Responsibility

To encourage, enable, and support the taking of personal responsibility in others, first realize that personal responsibility and thus self-leadership are innate in every human being. Responsibility is not just a character trait (nor is the lack of it a character flaw). It is a mental process that operates in everyone in predicable ways. This mental process, The Responsibility Process, described in detail in the next chapter, regulates how we choose to avoid or take responsibility. And, as reviewed in the previous section, we also understand quite a bit about how our actions can drive out feelings of personal responsibility in our offspring, the classroom, teams, organizations, and elsewhere. This means that responsibility can be systematically observed, taught, learned, practiced, and supported. Anyone can learn to master responsibility. And anyone can develop responsibility in a team, a family, a church, a school, or a work culture.

To encourage responsibility in others, we can

- grant them maximum autonomy so that they can take responsibility;

- allow them to make mistakes, self-correct, and learn instead of preventing their failure or rescuing them; and

- stop saving them from challenging trials so that they can experience natural consequences that allow for reflection and learning.

These are basic. There are many other principles we can understand and act on, which we will explore in coming chapters. For now, notice that if we want others to take responsibility, then we want to recognize their natural ability to respond by allowing high degrees of autonomy and non-intrusion. The opposite—lots of commands, controls, evaluations, and corrections—conditions people to become dependent on authority, to not think for themselves, and to then find freedom unsettling.

Responsibility Practice

Think of a time when an authority figure in your life accepted you unconditionally as a powerful learner allowing you the freedom to work things out and choose your own way. How might that have elevated levels of personal responsibility in you?

Think of a time when you accepted others unconditionally as powerful learners allowing them the freedom to figure things out and choose their own way. How might that have elevated levels of personal responsibility in them?

How to Make Accountability Unnecessary

When levels of ownership and personal responsibility are high in a team or organization, then accountability systems can be lightweight and simple because we don't need layers of watchers and heavy controls to know that people are producing results that matter. The level of engagement, ownership, and activity is obvious. The rate of productivity and goal achievement is high and also obvious. Self-leadership, self-organization, and self-direction is high. The freedom, power, and choice to say yes and no is critical. In such a system, if you ask me whether something will be done by next Tuesday, and I say yes, you probably don't have to ask me again—I don't need you to hold me to account because I take responsibility for myself and my agreements. If I did not think I could do what you request by next Tuesday, then I would say so. Transparency and ownership replaces the need for heavyweight performance management systems.

This is what high-performance systems look like. People taking responsibility eliminates the need for holding others to account. It is refreshing.

Responsibility Practice

Think of a relationship of yours where there are legitimate performance expectations, and yet the levels of personal responsibility are so high that seldom does one party feel the need to call out the other. Consider why it works so well without a heavy accountability system. Then, consider how you might replicate it in your other relationships.

Summary

To encourage us to think about personal responsibility in everyday life, this chapter looked at the issue of language and meaning for *accountability* and *responsibility*. We learned that these words are used interchangeably and are used to mean lots of different things such as admitting mistakes, making better choices, and apologizing.

I suggested that all the various meanings could be categorized into two broad meanings:

- Expectations of performance in a relationship

- Internal feelings of ownership

I also offered my preference for using *accountability* to refer to performance expectations and *responsibility* to refer to internal feelings of ownership. In an effort to be consistent, this is the language used throughout the remainder of the book.

Then the chapter turned to the leadership dynamics of accountability and responsibility. I observed that responsibility—either the taking of it or the avoidance of it—is a more powerful dynamic than accountability practices. I suggest that leaders of all types will benefit from placing greater understanding and focus on how to invite and allow people to take responsibility, than on how to manage accountabilities.

This is the end of part I. To put the idea of personal responsibility in perspective and set the stage for taking, leading, and coaching responsibility, part I discussed personal responsibility in everyday life. In chapter 1 "What Is Personal Responsibility?" we skipped across recorded history sampling treatments of personal responsibility from philosophy, psychology, religion, and government. In chapter 2, "Responsibility ≠ Accountability," we looked at the ambiguity and confusion around the use of the words "responsibility" and "accountability."

Up next, part II offers three tools that promise to help you take, lead, and coach personal responsibility, starting in chapter 3, "The Responsibility Process." It will help us understand accountability and responsibility so much better than we have previously.

Part II

Three Tools for Understanding and Practicing Responsibility

3

The Responsibility Process

When things go wrong, people blame. Not only do we blame, we also justify or make excuses. Frequently we feel ashamed or guilty and blame ourselves, mumbling self-deriding phrases like "I suck." And often we feel trapped in a commitment we can't change or get out of, so we feel obligated to be somebody we don't want to be, do something we don't want to do, and put up with having something we don't want to have. And as if all of that isn't enough, we do our best to park the problem, hiding it away in our mental closet and trying to pretend it doesn't matter. We say "whatever" with that breathy whine indicating acquiescence without ownership.

And sometimes we take a more resourceful view of the problem. We see how we can take ownership of it and free ourselves of the angst or upset.

The Responsibility Process

Welcome to The Responsibility Process, the first of three tools for understanding and practicing responsibility. This chapter is devoted to The Responsibility Process. Chapters 4 and 5 offer the second and third tools.

I just introduced you to each of the stages of The Responsibility Process, moving from Lay Blame to Responsibility.

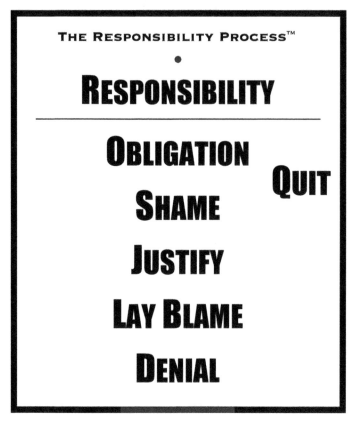

Figure 3.1. *The Responsibility Process.*

A series of mental states connected together in a mostly stepwise dynamic, The Responsibility Process (shown in figure 3.1) gets triggered by anxiety, frustration, or upset—even tiny ones. The Responsibility Process shows how we think about things that are bothering us. It shows how we process thoughts about cause and effect, about taking or avoiding responsibility for a problem. It brings us awareness of the self-talk going on in our heads when we are upset about something. That something could be internal and personal or it could be external, in our environment, or in our relationship to another person. Whatever it is, it is always unwanted, and negative, so we feel limited, constrained, and blocked from having what we want. We'd rather not be thinking about it (but the anxiety triggers it).

The pattern of the mental states, or stages, is predictable, hence the order. And each of the mental states serves up its own cause-and-effect logic for the problem. You can get stuck in any mental state around a problem for a moment, minute, day, month, year, decade, or lifetime. Or you can get off of it in which case you graduate to the next mental state above it. When something else goes wrong, The Responsibility Process gets triggered again and you start anew at the bottom.

In the mental states below the line (Denial, Lay Blame, Justify, Shame, Obligation, Quit), we cope with problems and we talk, talk, talk about them, or obsess internally and even lose sleep, but we never solve them from these mental positions. Above the line (Responsibility) we grow to overcome problems. They resolve and never come back, making us a freer and more powerful human being. When you understand this, you want to learn how to own and resolve everything that for you feels like a problem.

In this chapter we answer these important questions:

- How do problems trigger The Responsibility Process?

- What is the cause-and-effect logic of each mental state?

- How do you move between states?

- How does The Responsibility Process change our understanding of personal responsibility?

For the remainder of the book, when I refer to these mental states I will capitalize their names (Denial, Lay Blame, Justify, Shame, Obligation, Quit, and Responsibility). This will help us avoid confusion between talking generally about responsibility, and talking specifically about operating from the mental position of Responsibility.

At this point, I want to alert you to a possibility. While learning about The Responsibility Process, you may be reminded of a lingering upset or limitation somewhere in your life (we all have them). When that happens, feeling defensive or resistant is a normal coping response. Notice it, then let it be (you will learn more about why in the next chapter), or let it go.

You see, The Responsibility Process teaches us that you, and I, and everyone we know, are fully equipped both to take responsibility and to avoid responsibility for every experience in our lives. It teaches us that responsibility isn't just a character trait that some people have and others don't, but instead that it is a mechanism in our minds that we use all day every day to either succumb to problems, or to overcome them. And you and I succumb to a lot of problems, even though we are good "responsible" people. The Responsibility Process also illustrates that gulf of a difference between being responsible and taking 100 percent responsibility presented in the introduction. As you learn about The Responsibility Process in this chapter, you will probably recognize yourself. You might even cringe and think *ouch, I do that.* That's okay because it is likely true, and the truth is always okay to face. It is The Responsibility Process at work. That ouch signal is useful. Noticing it is a move toward mastery.

Responsibility Practice

Should you find yourself feeling defensive or resistant while reading this chapter, I invite you to (a) notice it, then (b) let it be—allow it to perturb you without having to take immediate action, or (c) let it go. You may even want to identify a current frustration, upset, or anxiety—either something recent or something that has bothered you for some time. You can carry it with you as a personal example as you read this chapter.

How Do Problems Trigger
The Responsibility Process?

You are dressed in your finest business suit for your big presentation to the board. And then it happens, you bump somebody in the hall on the way to the meeting and, as you are taking a sip of your latte, the paper cup slams into your face, its plastic lid pops off, and before you can stop it, two-thirds of the latte are soaked into the front of your finery, all the way from your neck to your waist.

You don't laugh this off.

"Oh expletive!" is the first thing out of your mouth. Then with that accusing look of I-can't-believe-you-did-that on your face, you turn to glare at the chump who bumped into you.

That's how problems trigger The Responsibility Process.

Here's a fuller explanation of what happened. You were in motion toward a goal (literally, in motion!). You had a serious investment of time, energy, and preparation for this important meeting. Then something happened that blocked your motion, something you neither anticipated nor liked. We call it an "oh, s___t." Or we call it an "oh no," an "uh oh," an "oh crap," or a "nooooo!" In your mind (the place that makes attributions of cause and effect), something is wrong. What's wrong? While the answer is obvious—you are covered with espresso and milk, not a pretty sight—there is another explanation. At that moment, there is a significant conflict in your mind between what you want, and what you have. What you want is to arrive at the meeting looking good. What you have is completely counter to that.

This internal conflict—between what you want and what you have—is the source of anxiety. When you are in motion toward a goal, and you get stopped, then you have a *problem*. This is technical language for those of us who study and practice responsibility. When we have something we don't want, or want something we don't think we can have, mentally we experience it as a problem. We also call it an *upset, angst, frustration,* or *anxiety.* You know the feeling.

This is the trigger for The Responsibility Process. The trigger is the same for all upsets large and small. Anytime you are making progress toward what you want, and then you-know-what happens, you have an internal conflict between what you want and what you have. You have an upset, and that's a problem.

It doesn't matter whether it is spilled coffee or a river spilling over its banks and flooding your home. The mental response to something going wrong is the same.

In the next section we'll look at what happens next.

Responsibility Practice

Consider how many times a day The Responsibility Process in your mind is triggered by an upset large or small. To answer that question ask, How many times a day do things go wrong? How many things have gone wrong already today? Did it start with an alarm going off while you were comfortably snoozing and your next thought was *oh no, I don't want to get up*?

Wouldn't it be great if you could instantly recognize this trigger and know how to get to a totally resourceful state of mind?

The Cause-and-Effect Logic of Each Mental State

Our first thought when something goes wrong is *Who did this to me?* And then our mind immediately pictures that person.

Lay Blame

How often does this happen: A project or assignment didn't go well. The team scrambles into a meeting. The manager asks, "What happened?!" Then, rather than discover what happened, people start suggesting who caused the problem:

- "The client didn't clearly tell us about their needs."

- "The other team didn't deliver their dependencies."

- "Our vendor missed a deadline."

At the end of the meeting, the leader declares *who* caused the problem. Everyone breathes a big sigh of relief. While walking out, someone says to you, "I'm sure glad that wasn't my fault."

You've just heard the language of Lay Blame, and it happens every day in meetings, classrooms, kitchens, and conversations everywhere. The moment something goes wrong, our mind begins a hyperactive search for cause and effect. The first place the mind visits in The Responsibility Process is the mental state of Lay Blame. There, the mind looks for the culprit who did this to us. If we can Lay Blame on someone, then we can direct our upset and anxiety toward that person.

They are the problem.

You've probably been taught your entire life to not blame. Indeed most societies teach that blaming is a victim mentality where you are giving your power away to another. And I bet you teach your charges that they should not blame. Yet Lay Blame is still our first feeling and thought when things go wrong.

So does that mean we are lousy learners?

I don't think so. The Responsibility Process is so observable in everyone that I am quite sure it is hardwired, part of our basic makeup. It is how our minds first respond to upset.

It is common to criticize people who blame. We say they are bad or wrong for blaming. But The Responsibility Process shows that there is nothing wrong with them since they are acting on their natural thought processes. We don't blame because we are bad or wrong, we blame because we are human. We are operating normally—according to The Responsibility Process, just not as resourcefully as we could be operating.

Here are some important things to remember about Lay Blame:

- Lay Blame is a natural mental state. It's common and predictable.

- Everyone feels the impulse to Lay Blame on others when things go wrong. I believe we are hardwired to do it. It's part of our genetic makeup.

- Lay Blame is triggered by our emotions, specifically by our anxiety about a problem. It is not triggered by our intellect (although we apply our intellect to be particularly cunning or persuasive as we Lay Blame).

However, Lay Blame is a mental trap. Here's why: When we're in the mental state of Lay Blame, we tell ourselves that we are powerless victims, clearly not at fault. We tell ourselves that someone else caused our problem. It's all their fault. We assume that for our problem to go away, someone else must change.

So the cause-effect logic in Lay Blame is that you occupy the position of *effect*, and the object of your blame occupies the position of *cause*.

In the cause-effect equation then, the cause is outside of you, it's external. Problem solving from this mental state and its logic can only find one solution—that person must change for your problem to go away.

A few years ago, Big Semiconductor Inc.'s (real story, made up names) executive vice president of manufacturing, along with the executive vice president of sales, and a dozen of their team members visited their customer, Huge Automaker, at their offices in Detroit. This was referred to as the annual dog-and-pony show where the supplier for a $50 million account reports to the customer how wonderful everything is going. At the conclusion of the presentations, the executive from Huge Automaker said: "Huge Automaker is not nearly as thrilled with Big Semiconductor Inc. as you are with yourselves. We have a list of thirteen specific areas that require improvement. We'll give you six months to show substantial improvement in these thirteen areas or you will be de-sourced from the account."

I did not know *de-source* was a word. But I knew what they meant by it, and it wasn't good. Losing a $50 million account to one of your competitors is a $100 million swing in market share. Not good.

When they got back home, the executives from Big Semiconductor Inc. organized a series of meetings to consider their strategy. As the executive vice president of manufacturing later told it, for the first two months they found themselves in meetings blaming the customer for not knowing what they were talking about. "We have the finest quality programs and the best fabs in the world," Big Semiconductor Inc.'s executives exclaimed to one another. "Surely Huge Automaker has to see that!!" they snuffed. Then one day the executive vice president found himself staring at the list of thirteen specific demands and he experienced a mental shift. He thought to himself "Hey, this is a menu, and the customer is placing an order. All we have to do is what they ask—make substantive improvements in each of these areas—and there is an implied contract to continue doing business. What are we waiting for!?"

How did this conclude? Very well actually. Big Semiconductor Inc. formed a large cross-organizational customer-focus team to address the thirteen areas and save the $50 million account. A year later they earned distinction as one of Huge Automaker's top suppliers. Two years later they earned a much larger piece of Huge Automaker's business, nearly tripling the size of the account.

Looking back, Big Semiconductor Inc.'s EVP of manufacturing is amazed at the two months he wasted blaming the customer for their view of the business. He wondered how much more progress they could have made if they had used all six months given them to show substantial progress instead of wasting the first two months and leaving only four months for actual problem solving.

So this story begs the question: How do we move on from the mental state of Lay Blame? We exit Lay Blame the moment we reject the need for a scapegoat. We simply refuse to blame others. Or put another way, when, as Responsibility practitioners, we notice ourselves having thoughts of blame, we choose to immediately stop blaming. It sounds straightforward, and it is; however, it can be quite challenging due to our conditioned mental habits. We remain stuck in Lay Blame, coping with, rather than solving, the problem until we become aware of the trap and make a conscious choice to reject it.

The lesson then is to pay attention to our own thoughts, language, and behaviors when we are upset or frustrated. We like to say "every upset is an opportunity to learn." I know when I feel anger toward a teammate—and especially when I want to chew someone out—well, that's when I know I am in Lay Blame. Realizing it is a signal to ask myself whether I really want to remain in that mental state. *No* I think to myself, and I stop blaming. In the "Justify" section we'll look at what happens next.

Responsibility Practice

To reflect on Lay Blame, ask yourself these questions:

- Am I in the mental state of Lay Blame right now for some situation in my life, relationships, or work?
- How is holding on to blame keeping me from making new and powerful choices and being free of that problem?
- How much time and energy do I pour into blaming?
- How could I catch myself blaming and get off of it so that I can work on solving a problem instead of coping?

Justify

When we stop our Lay Blame behavior toward others, we move to the mental state of Justify. Justify is a little different from Lay Blame. In Justify we blame circumstances instead of people. We tell ourselves stories that justify why we have the problem. If we can't—or refuse to—Lay Blame on another person for our problems, then we seek another excuse.

Before I explain Justify, I want us to make a switch. Remember earlier in this chapter when you were walking along and spilled a latte down the front of your suit, which upset you and sent you to Lay Blame? Lets look at this spilled latte scenario and The Responsibility Process again from another viewpoint. We're going to take you out of the story and replace you with a young professional. To refresh, she was dressed in her best business suit, on the way to a critical opportunity to present to the big bosses, when she bumped someone while drinking her latte and the cup emptied covering her from neck to waist. What was her first response? She whirled around to glare at the person who had so rudely bumped her. Only no one was there. Realizing this, she next spied the four-foot tall cubicle wall that defined the isle as you come around the corner. Her elbow had hit the cube wall, which in turn caused her to push the coffee cup into her face, allowing the contents to spill. "Damn cubes!" she blurted out.

When we stop our thoughts of blame, we graduate to Justify. Yes, we graduate, as in, move to the next level. If you look back to figure 3.1 of The Responsibility Process earlier in this chapter, you will see that the words are mostly stacked, one on top of another. When you exit a mental state lower on the list, you graduate to, or land in, the next mental state up. It is quite predicable.

In Justify we are sure that circumstances caused our problem. And it is those circumstances to which we direct our upset ("damn cube wall!").

Here are a few examples of what Justify can sound like in an organization:

- "We're stuck with outdated technology."

- "Our processes are overly bureaucratic."

- "Why bother? Nothing ever changes around here."

Justify is a pernicious mental state. It is so active in our lives and work that we don't realize how much coping we are doing instead of problem solving—until we become attuned to it. We don't realize how much of our energy we are dumping into Justify. We are especially good at justifying together to cope with our shared anxieties. Consider the number-one justify that I hear in client organizations: "That's just the way it is around here," followed by heads nodding in agreement.

When we're stuck in the mental state of Justify, we actually believe that we're victims of the situation. We tell ourselves—and others—that we're powerless to change the situation. We say, "There's nothing I can do." This concerns me because I see otherwise brilliant, highly educated, outwardly successful people invest hours, days, and years coping instead of growing—and commiserating with each other in meetings, at lunch, at the gym, and especially at happy hour while complaining about "how it is."

Here's an important clue. If you have ongoing frustration and complaints about some situation, you may be hanging out in Justify. If you and your spouse somehow get a kick out of complaining about your neighborhood, schools, homeowners association, etc., you might be coping with a problem instead of solving it. If you and your colleagues at work find yourselves returning time and again to the same complaints about the management, the culture, the processes, suppliers, customers, or the structure, take a look at how much energy you are investing in remaining powerless against the circumstances.

Remember, if you are having an ouch moment that I predicted in the first Responsibility Practice section in this chapter, consider letting it be or letting it go. Have some compassion for yourself. There is nothing wrong with you. You are normal. You just aren't in as resourceful a mental state as you could be, and before reading this you didn't know. So you coped. The great news is that now you are developing new mental strategies by reading this book.

Let's look at the cause-and-effect logic of Justify.

In the mental state of Justify, there is just one logic available to us, I call this a "logic box." In Justify, we see ourselves in the position of effect—i.e., the problem is happening to us. And we see the circumstances—e.g., the weather, traffic, economy, or business culture—in the position of cause. This leaves only one premise—that for our problem to go away, the circumstances must change. We tell ourselves the circumstances must change before our problem will resolve and we can be happy and productive.

So how long will we wait for the world to change for us? A month? What if the circumstances never change? If we passively wait for the situation to change, then we'll continue to feel ongoing frustration and upset.

And maybe we prefer the certainty of grabbing for the easy excuse to the uncertainty of actually owning the real source of the problem and facing it.

So, how can we escape the mental state of Justify?

Again, as we learned in the section on Lay Blame, the solution is conceptually simple. But it's not easy. To escape Justify, we want to become vitally aware of the stories we are telling ourselves. We must recognize that we're positioning ourselves as powerless. When we realize this, we usually choose to stop justifying for that problem.

The difference between feeling powerless and powerful is an idea based in emotion. The Responsibility Process teaches us that we have far more power over our lives, work, success, and satisfaction than we usually give ourselves credit for. This recognition allows us to escape the Justify mindset, and it moves us one step closer to Responsibility.

Recently I faced a daunting challenge. I had just ended a business relationship with a near-genius of a consultant. He had done amazing things to help us grow Partnerwerks; however, he repeatedly violated values that define who we are and what we stand for. It took me over a year to see it, but by the time I did, we had developed significant relationship problems in the company and with our clients. Once I saw this the decision to separate was easy and swift. Violating values contributes far more harm than genius expertise can add.

Now I had a problem. We were in motion on a growth strategy, and I felt the skills this person brought were critical. And now he was gone. "Woe is me," I commiserated. "How would I ever replace this amazing skill set?" I agonized over this question lying awake in bed, while driving, while sitting on airplanes, and even while preparing to give a keynote speech at a large conference. I was in Justify for about two weeks! You see, I was sure this person's skill sets were so scarce that I could never replace them. I was doomed. The circumstances were more powerful than I was.

Then one day I asked myself, *What if I am just telling myself a story—like a movie that I wrote in my head and watch over and over?* The story vanished. I had convinced myself I was a powerless victim. I was trapped in Justify. I had accepted the story that it would be impossible to find the person with the skills I needed. My mental state made it so true! I made myself powerless. As soon as I rejected the story, my angst lifted. I felt joy immediately. And I thought to myself, yes, replacing these skills might be challenging, but it will be impossible as long as I assume the world is conspiring against me when I know it isn't. So, I rolled up my sleeves and went to work. I immediately made two phone calls to access my network. In three days, I had met two potential candidates. I felt great.

When we reject the story about how we're powerless to change our circumstances, we leave Justify. Guess what happens when we get off of the mental state of Justify? We'll answer that in the next section.

Responsibility Practice

What are some of your stories that provide an excuse for things not being as you want? Is it about

- the weather and your mood?
- the traffic and being irate?
- your busyness and being consistently late?
- the company culture and being dissatisfied at work?
- the economy and not making a living wage?

Start listening for Justify. Doing so will move you toward mastery.

Shame

I felt bad for a split second after I recognized the whopper of a story I was telling myself about how I would never be able to find someone with the skill set and values that I sought—even though I had not tried. I went straight to the mental state of Shame. The good news was that this lasted for only a split second, literally less than a second. But I marked that moment when I both discovered my Justify and briefly visited Shame. Why mark the moment as memorable? Because it was a significant win as an application of my responsibility practice. It's where I released the pent-up tension, the want-versus-have internal conflict I had been feeding for a couple of weeks. I remember the scene. I was in the lobby of a ballroom in a major Washington DC hotel preparing to give a speech. I can picture it clearly in my mind now.

And why, you ask, did I spend such a short time in Shame? Well, for one, I've had a responsibility practice for twenty-four years, and I'm pretty good at catching myself in these mental states and letting them go. I caught myself and decided I didn't need to waste any more time beating myself up. Remember, we can stay in these states around a problem for a second or a lifetime, or we can let them go. The surprise for me was not the short time in Shame but the long time in Justify!

Here's another short vignette showing how we graduate from Lay Blame to Justify to Shame. I once lost my car keys. I first thought someone took them, but no one had been in my office since I drove to work. That knocked me off of Lay Blame. Then my mind offered the excuse *I had a million things going on, no wonder I forgot where I put my keys.* When I realized that was a story of Justify, I rejected it. Then I became really aggravated at myself for losing my keys. I actually said, "What a dolt I am!"

Let's check in on the spilled latte scene visited earlier in this chapter. If you recall, our star of the story is walking through her office building to a power meeting where she will be the center of attention. She's wearing her finest suit, $350 designer heels, and well, you recall what happened with the latte as she turned the corner. A few seconds after she blurts out

"Damn cube wall!" her closest and funniest friend at work quips with a grin, "You're really going to blame the wall?" You can see a noticeable shift in her mental energy revealed in her face as it distorts from outward anger to inner remorse. She sighs, looks at her friend, and announces, "What a klutz I am."

When we exit Justify, we land in Shame, just like the star of our story illustrated with her klutz comment.

The first two positions of The Responsibility Process—Lay Blame and Justify—are externally focused. When we enter the mental state of Shame, we're sure that we are the problem. Thus, Shame occurs when we stop externalizing our problem. Our focus turns inward. So in Shame, we're simply Laying Blame on self.

Let's examine the cause-and-effect logic in this logic box of Shame. In Shame you see yourself in both positions of cause and effect—but not in a healthy and resourceful way. You think *I did this to me. Ugh.*

Listen to the language of Shame:

- "I'm not smart enough."

- "I'm such a dummy."

- "I'm not skilled enough."

- "I didn't try hard enough."

- "I don't deserve success."

- "I suck."

The premise in Shame is that we lack what we need. We think we don't have what it takes, or we think we deserve to have the problem because we should not have dared to do the thing that led to the problem. We tell ourselves we're feeling bad because we lack something AND that we deserve to feel bad because of it! We're not only ashamed but guilty too.

The Responsibility Process

Many people, even highly skilled professionals, get trapped in and controlled by the mental state of Shame. They tell themselves that no matter how smart or successful they have been, they're never really good enough.

How could this be? Think about it, in many societies, when people express shame, they receive praise for "taking responsibility." That's right, we have been conditioned to land and stay in Shame when we make mistakes or have problems. It may be called "taking responsibility" but The Responsibility Process shows that it's a false responsibility. Why? Because we still have the problem, we still have the anxiety, and we are still coping rather than owning and solving the problem. In Shame we are our own problem. And we get to remain our own problem as long as we stay in this mental state.

Let's explore the true difference between Shame and Responsibility with two scenarios. Imagine attending two back-to-back after-action review meetings, A and B. In meeting A, someone stands up in front of the group and declares, "I caused the problem. Blame me. I've got big shoulders and can take the hit." All attendees let out a short sigh of relief (that a single point of accountability has been identified and they're not it). And then everyone smiles at the person in front of the room and says, "Good boy, he's taking responsibility."

In meeting B someone also stands in front of the group and declares, "I caused the problem." But instead of espousing his self-pity he goes on to say, "Now, here is when we caught it. Here's what we did to stop the bleeding. Here's what we did to clean up the mess we caused for others. And here's what we've learned about why I would make that mistake in the first place. We've communicated this to the other team members so they won't repeat my blunder. Now I'd like your help determining what other amends are called for."

So which of the two meetings, A or B, demonstrated Shame and which demonstrated Responsibility? Most people recognize meeting A as Shame and meeting B as true Responsibility. The actor in meeting A showed self-pity and not much more. In meeting B the actor took ownership and offered a complete confession that eliminated any need for castigation by another. There was also correction, learning, relationship repair, information sharing, and most importantly, the self-acknowledgment of being human (and humans make mistakes). The problem solver was operating from the mental state of Responsibility, saying in essence, I am an agent both in causing and overcoming problems in my life. I made a mistake, and the sooner I get over myself the sooner I can get to making amends.

Shame is a powerful mental trap that masquerades in too many societies as a virtue. This is an important lesson from The Responsibility Process. Our cultural norms generally agree with what The Responsibility Process teaches us about Lay Blame and Justify. We consistently teach that you should not blame and make excuses. But then our culture rewards Shame. We condition our charges to be good, feel bad when they err, and if you let down another person, by all means act contrite and say sorry. We tell them they are being responsible when they feel bad for getting into a problem that they contributed to. We are culturally addicted to this mental state of Shame. It permeates our lives, work, and relationships. It keeps smart, educated, otherwise successful people stuck in lives they don't want.

And it doesn't need to remain this way.

How can we get out of Shame? The solution is simple and, again, not easy. First, we want to notice that we are blaming ourselves. Then, we make a new choice. We choose to stop laying blame on ourselves. In future chapters I will give you more tools to support you in doing this. For now, I'll offer you a question that works pretty well for a lot of people when they find themselves in Shame. The question is this: How long do you deserve to beat yourself up for being human? Or a variation: How long do you want to hang out in Shame? Additionally, you can remind yourself that you won't solve the problem from that mental state. You will only cope. So the sooner you get off of Shame the better.

In the next section we'll discover what happens when we leave Shame.

Responsibility Practice

How have you been rewarded or reinforced throughout your life for demonstrating Shame—and people called it "taking responsibility"?

Have you shamed others, eliciting a response of Shame, and you called it "taking responsibility"?

Notice our societal norms around *being responsible* (i.e., being good in the eyes of another) versus truly *taking responsibility*. Think about, and listen for, the use of *responsibility* for the coping states. "I'm responsible, I'll take the hit" says responsible, but this expresses Shame. "The front-line employees are responsible for missing quota" says responsible, but this expresses Lay Blame. The word *responsibility* is used to communicate all the various attributions of cause and effect. So realize it is not about the word itself but about the feeling-tone of the mental state.

Obligation

When you leave the mental state of Shame, you land in the mental state of Obligation. Obligation is the mental state of feeling trapped or burdened in your life, work, or relationships. In Obligation, you are sure you have no choice, you have to:

- do something you don't want to do,

- be somebody you don't want to be, or

- have something you don't want to have.

Do means action, *be* means identity, and *have* means experience. These are the three ways we think about our existence as humans. An example of having to do something you don't want to do could be having to attend that stupid meeting (or go to school, or do grocery shopping). An example of being somebody you don't want to be could be violating your personal values to satisfy the demands of a superior to remain employed (or hiding your true feelings to fit in). And an example of having something you don't want to have might be an impossible calendar schedule that you don't control.

Obligation is the mental state of "have to, but don't want to."

Let me share a personal example. One day I was annoyed that I "had to" push some urgent work aside and accompany my sons to their after-school activities. My mind was focused on the work, and I wanted to keep it that way. With the kid activities, I felt I *had to* do something I *didn't want to do,* and I resented it. Then I caught myself grumbling internally and growling at my boys. Because of my responsibility practice and my commitment to responsibility, I caught myself in Obligation, and I stopped. How? I refused to feel obligated. Period. I forgave myself for being human. Then I silently asked myself what I wanted. The answer came immediately: I had signed up for this lifelong activity of being a dad, and I truly wanted to be a dad at that moment and enjoy my sons. I also wanted them to see me as a dad who cared about them more than I cared about my work. My resentment vanished, I set aside the work for later, and I had a great time with my sons.

Over the past twenty-five years, I have shared The Responsibility Process while mentoring young people who were just starting their careers and with senior executives who were at the height of their careers. I have found that the Obligation mindset is a particularly expensive trap that people find themselves in nearly constantly. Obligation imprisons the brightest and most ambitious people and keeps them stuck.

The Responsibility Process

Most people confuse Obligation with Responsibility. In fact, in the earlier example, if I had confessed to my wife that I didn't really want to engage in dad duties that afternoon, she would have been culturally appropriate to say, "Christopher you have a responsibility to your sons." Now substitute the words *obligation* and *duty* for the word responsibility in that sentence:

- "Christopher you have an obligation to your sons."

- "Christopher you have a duty to your sons."

All three forms of the sentence ring true. Each one says I am morally obligated to do the right thing as a dad, and if I don't then I am not being a good dad and husband. But here is the thing. Even though we use the terms *obligation* and *responsibility* interchangeably, there is a gulf of a difference between the mental states of Obligation and Responsibility—between being a good person and taking 100 percent responsibility. In Obligation we feel trapped, burdened, and that we have no choice. In Responsibility we feel free, powerful, and "at choice" (i.e., we have one or more choices so we do not feel burdened or trapped in a situation of "no choice.").

Our cultural trance teaches us and constantly reinforces that keeping our commitments is a good thing, even if we don't like it. Society teaches us that good, responsible people do what they are supposed to do, even if they don't like it. "Suck it up," we say. "Just do it." "No excuses." "Quit complaining." "Do you want them to think you don't care?" "Then do the right thing."

And that "right thing" means to appear to others to be good, to be responsible—to be morally virtuous—by being, doing, and having exactly what we don't want!

Don't get me wrong, I have nothing against obligations and commitments. Business and life depends on our ability to make and keep commitments. However Obligation, the mental state, is a feeling state. It does not refer to the commitment itself but to how you feel about your commitment. Don't confuse making a commitment with how you feel about that commitment.

Think of the difference between an obligation or commitment, and the mental state of Obligation this way: Let's say we accept an invitation to a meeting. That's a commitment. If we go to the meeting, and we are mentally present, on purpose, and actively engaged, that's great. However, if we reluctantly go to the meeting, we show up in the mental state of Obligation. We resent being there. Our interest and motivation are low, and we may be at least partially checked out.

When we're in the mental state of Obligation, there's a conflict between what we want and what we have. This conflict produces stress and anxiety. It prevents us from taking true ownership and experiencing Responsibility. We can hear this tension clearly in the language of Obligation. Listen for language that communicates a burden, entrapment, or having no choice:

- "I have no choice; I have to go to this stupid meeting."

- "I have to complete that pile of paperwork."

- "I have to go to my in-laws for the holidays."

"Have to" is the language of Obligation. What goes unsaid is the silent "don't want to," and yet it is completely clear when you become aware of it. In case you are wondering if you might be experiencing some of this Obligation mindset, let's turn these earlier examples into a pop quiz:

- Do you have some boring and valueless meeting you *have to* regularly attend?

- Do you have some meaningless paperwork you *have to* complete?

- Do you *have to* go to your in-laws for the holidays?

In each of these examples, our true desires are in conflict with our perceived reality. And that tension produces low motivation, low engagement, and resentment. These are clear signals that we are in Obligation.

People frequently ask me: "Christopher, what's wrong with Obligation? Isn't that how we design roles at work? We assign roles and hold people accountable (obligated)." My answer is twofold. First, there is nothing wrong with Obligation. It is a natural human mental state like each of the others. Secondly, it is a tremendously unresourceful and costly mental state.

There are two huge and obvious costs or taxes when people operate from Obligation. First, in Obligation our performance is barely adequate to get a pass. Smart, ambitious people perform at the bare minimum required to survive the perceived trap. We produce unsatisfying results. Think about that horrible meeting you have to attend. How present and engaged are you in the meeting? I know, not very engaged at all.

Now, estimate the loss to productivity when you operate from Obligation. Choose any number you think makes sense from 0 percent to 100 percent, then multiply that lost productivity across your teams, departments, organizations, and industries—all sectors, all professions. The Obligation mindset produces an enormous and totally unnecessary tax on performance at work. It affects the top line and carries all the way to the bottom line.

The second outrageous cost of the Obligation mindset is resentment. Resentment is a mental virus that grows as you cope with having what you don't want. It sucks mental energy, directs your angst toward the things that you believe have you trapped—family, work, boss, career, mortgage, etc., and prevents you from perceiving cause and effect clearly, and then taking Responsibility. You see things in a negative light and may be cynical and sarcastic. You attract others who are feeling the same resentment and together amplify the cynicism and sarcasm, which are harmful to engagement, teamwork, and collaboration.

Therefore, Obligation becomes devastatingly expensive to you, your team, the organization, and society. Obligation is a multitrillion-dollar status-quo drag on happiness and productivity in our society. Some individuals and teams spend their entire career trapped in an Obligation mindset, especially if they are working without passion or purpose in an unfulfilling job that does not suit them. And all because they want to be good responsible people.

Once again we see that being generally responsible citizens does not mean that we are operating from the mental state of Responsibility. According to our cultural trance, you can hang out in Shame to show that you are a responsible person. You can also hang out in Obligation while looking responsible by societal standards.

We will remain stuck in Obligation until we refuse to let ourselves feel trapped by our roles, jobs, relationships, or circumstances. It is a mental position of no power, no freedom, and no choice (i.e., I have to, I have no choice). That's why one of my mantras is that I never do anything I don't want to do. It reminds me that my legs are not in shackles and my hands are not bound. Whatever I am doing that I am grumbling about is still a choice that I am making, even if I don't want to own it. The moment I own that I am choosing—that at some level I must want to do it—is the moment I find the power to change.

Remember, the commitment itself is not the issue. The issue is (a) how you feel about the commitment, and (b) your ability to make commitments that you will enjoy keeping. People who practice and master Responsibility don't avoid commitments, instead they continually shape their life choices to make commitments they love keeping. People who practice responsibility at high levels make very clear choices about yes and no.

And don't kid yourself that the mental entrapment of Obligation only happens to workers and not to the elite. People at every strata of society get trapped in Obligation. I was working with the board of directors of an exciting company. At a break in our meetings, when he could speak to me in private, a successful and wealthy businessman who was on the board of directors approached me, shared that he was also on the board of regents for Huge State University System (a pseudonym of course). Then, to show that he identified with the Obligation mindset I had just introduced him to, he confessed how he loathed having to go to next weekend's Huge State University System regents meeting. Had to go! Poor thing. The regents were meeting in the finest hotel in the state—Michelin-rated restaurant; exquisite furnishings, oriental carpets; crystal, china, gold-plated silverware; vintage French champagne; and, of course, twenty-five-year-old single-cask scotch. Statewide, the place had the most professional staff of chefs, butlers, and other attendants. And this poor fellow is feeling burdened by having to put up with all of that. You and I imagine he must be nuts, until we realize that he is no different from us; he's just trapped in a different class of plush hand-cuffs. I surmise that whatever value he once thought he could contribute as a Huge State University System regent has been thwarted, and he now feels stuck in a role attending boring valueless meetings, biding his time until his tenure as a regent is up. Of course he could resign as a regent, right? Yes, just like you and I could resign from our dull roles. Oh, well when you look at it that way, you understand that what has him trapped is the same thing that may have us trapped. He doesn't want the consequences he imagines would accompany resigning. It might affect his business relationships, his political connections, or his personal relationships. So he sucks it up and does the "right thing" by spending his weekend as a mildly resentful low performer trapped in dull meetings surrounded by finery.

When we operate from Responsibility, as we will see in the next section, we get to examine our life, work, choices, and commitments. We may realize that our burdens are in fact things we can own in order to serve a higher purpose or goal—such as my earlier example about deciding I really did want to be a dad and participate happily in after-school activities.

Here's an example of owning something that feels like Obligation and making a new choice. I once worked with a leader who noticed that team members viewed huddle meetings with dread and dismay. They all felt that they "had to" attend this meeting. But because everyone attended out of Obligation, the meetings were boring, unfocused, and unproductive. The manager recognized the burden and gathered the team. She asked, "What could we do to turn this weekly meeting from a 'have to' into a 'want to'?" It worked. Soon, everyone was energized. The conversation was candid. Everyone offered ideas on how to improve the meeting—so people would want to show up and take ownership.

The feeling of being burdened by Obligation is simply a state of mind, a mental trap that we create for ourselves. In this mental state, we can't experience feeling free, powerful, and at choice. Yet, everything we do, everything we are, and everything we experience can be on purpose. The exit from Obligation is refusing to feel trapped. The more aware you become of your perceptions of cause and effect, the more you'll be able to help others become aware of their limiting, burdensome perceptions at home and at work!

Let's check in on our heroine and her upcoming presentation in her latte-stained suit. Refusing to stay in Shame, she thinks of an action she could take to feel better. "I know," she says, "I'll never walk and drink coffee again." This is a bit of a stretch, but it is Obligation, especially if she feels she can't have what she wants (i.e., a latte on the move), because of her new personal policy. Her policy still leaves her in a have-to-don't-want-to situation, producing anxiety, and the need to cope with it.

Responsibility Practice

Take a look at the areas of your life, work, and relationships where you frequently find yourself in Obligation. Suspend judgment about right or wrong, good or bad, or even possible or impossible (to change). Simply identify parts of your life, work, and relationships where you feel trapped, burdened, or in which you have to be, do, or have something you don't want.

Take this awareness forward as you read this book. The tools in the next two chapters will support you in freeing yourself, either by choosing to love the commitment, or by choosing to change it.

Responsibility

A thousand more thoughts rushed through her mind. *I can't go in there with latte down the front of my suit. I know—I'll feign illness and cancel the meeting. No wait, I'll trip and say I sprained my ankle and have to go to the emergency room. Or...*

Recognizing all of these thoughts as anxiety-driven avoidances of the truth, and knowing how to practice responsibility because she'd been mastering Responsibility for the past year, the talented junior executive stopped, took some slow deep breaths for a few moments, found her mental and emotional center even in the midst of the drama and anxiety, and asked herself silently "What do I want about this problem right now?" In a flash her truth came to her clearly, and she smiled, feeling free, powerful, and at choice—even with her soiled clothes. She wanted to shake off the accident, maybe even use the story as an icebreaker for the presentation, and go into that meeting and close the deal, now. *They are humans too*, she thought, smiling even more. *If they can't allow me a silly wardrobe mishap, and instead they allow my latte accessorizing to get in the way of business progress, then I'm on the wrong team.* She thought. *Let's do this.*

In the meeting, there was no justifying or sheepish self-loathing as so often happens when something is clearly out of place. She went straight to 100 percent owning it by saying, "Good morning ladies and gentleman. Yes, as you can see, on the way over here just now I tried tie-dying my suit with an overpriced coffee. What do you think? New office fashion? All right, enough of that as my suit and I will be fine. Now, let's consider the three key points of this proposal . . ."

What is Responsibility? Responsibility is a mental state that is open, spacious, free, and safe. You trust that you have sufficient intelligence, creativity, and resources to face whatever life brings. Where the other states are restrictive, this one is spacious, giving you room to think and explore. In the other states, you feel constrained or trapped, but in Responsibility you are free to choose and free from preconceived ideas about the problem or solution. You are free to reexamine what you want, free to just be. In the other states, especially Shame and Obligation, you are not safe. In Responsibility there is compassion and understanding, the foundation to a sense of safety with ourselves. This safety is necessary to confront uncertainties with courage (we will learn more about Confront as a key to Responsibility in the next chapter).

Responsibility is a mental state that you are completely equipped to access anytime. You were born with it. And you have accessed it thousands of times in your life. In fact, you have accessed it every time you have grown to overcome something that had been a challenging problem.

Responsibility is owning your power and ability to create, choose, and attract your reality. In fact, that is how we define Responsibility: "Owning your power and ability to create, choose, and attract your reality."

If you look at this definition in parts, it says we are always creating, choosing, and attracting our reality; we just aren't always owning it. In the other mental states, we aren't owning that we are creating, choosing, and attracting our reality. We are sure that our reality is imposed on us. In Responsibility, we own it.

There are other important differences. See the following table.

In Lay Blame, Justify, Shame, Obligation, Quit, and Denial	In Responsibility
Our reasoning is simplistic and restricted by the mental state.	We have available to us the entire complex probabilistic reasoning capabilities of our extraordinary mind.
Our logic is mechanical, looking at simplistic cause and effect.	Our logic is holistic, taking a systems view of all the interrelated elements in our lives, work, and relationships.
We are driven by anxiety.	We are pulled by what we truly want in life, at work, in relationships, both for the long term and for this situational problem moment right now.
We are fairly weak.	We are incredibly strong.
We are constrained by our reality.	We craft our reality.
We are victims.	We are agents.
We have problems that are more powerful than we are.	We know that we are more powerful than any problem we face.

Let's look at the phrase at the end of the definition: "choose, create, and attract your reality." By "your reality" I mean your subjective experience of life, your subjective reality. You could substitute "your experience" or even "your life." What is important here is that Responsibility isn't just about creating, choosing, and attracting the outer trappings of "success" but also about the inner experience of freedom, choice, and power, which is true success.

Some people have difficulty with the *attract* part of the definition of Responsibility. A few struggle with *create*. Most accept that we *choose*. So let's briefly look at all three words:

Choose. We have the power and ability to know and express our wants and desires through preferences and through identifying options or choices. For example, I want to experience excellent mental and physical health, so I choose a healthy diet, exercise, and sleep patterns.

We learn to make different choices by examining past choices to see how they worked out for us. I see a fairly linear cause-effect relationship in many choices and consequences. For example, I chose to stay up late last night, and this morning I am paying for it with tiredness and poor focus and attention.

Create. Create means to cause to come into being.[1] It can be a thing such as a product design, or a situation such as how good it feels to be a part of a well-functioning department. I see creating as a little more complex and less linear than a choice. It involves multiple choices over time. When we deliberately create a positive experience, it involves envisioning the end result to some degree, planning a series of choices, then experimenting and reflecting to arrive at the desired experience. You can see this in kids making a sand castle at the beach, a classroom teacher leading a class through a curriculum to a desired effect, or a team leader bringing a group together around a shared goal.

We also create unwanted experiences, usually unconsciously, by not perceiving or predicting the future consequences of a series of choices. For instance, by spending more than we make, we create a problem with our finances. If we are willing to own that we created that problem for ourselves, then we can examine the series of choices that lead to it, and we can learn to make new choices that turn the experience around.

Attract. Attract means to draw to you either by a physical force such as gravity or magnetism, by appealing to the emotions or senses, or by spiritual or mystical means. It is the spiritual or mystical means of attracting that many find dubious and others hold dear. When it comes to understanding and practicing responsibility, both beliefs are okay with me. You can build your responsibility practice with a purely experiential definition of *attract*.

I see *attract* as even more complex and less linear than *create*. So you may attract positive experiences and truly not realize how you are doing it, in which case you do not recognize your power and ability to attract. For instance, you may have a cheery disposition at work, and, as a result you attract lots of smiles, warm interactions, and colleagues who want to work with you. You might attribute the cause of this experience to the workplace when it may be as much about your own power and ability to attract positivity. You may also attract negative experiences and not know how you are doing that. I once knew a fellow who attracted (others would say caused) arguments in every meeting at work, no matter what the topic. To him, it was always the other person's fault for being so unprepared, ignorant, or just plain wrong. He felt he must correct them (in an invalidating way), and that led to an argument. He actually claimed that he did not enjoy arguing, that it made him unhappy, and did not understand why it always happened to him. If I am willing to look at a negative experience as something that I may have attracted, I can learn quite a bit about myself.

The Responsibility Process teaches us that we are far more powerful and able than we usually give ourselves credit for. How so? Let's do a simple mathematical thought problem. Remember that every time something goes wrong, big or small, and you get that internal conflict that generates anxiety, you automatically trigger The Responsibility Process in your mind. Let's say your mental circuits are coping right now with twenty-five problems such as:

- How can I get my low performer to be accountable?

- Are we going to ever get the house ready to sell?

- Will our kids be successful?

- How can I tell my boss I need a raise?

- What's our competition going to do when we launch our marketing campaign?

- How come I can't fit into my jeans?

- When is my spouse going to do his share?

- When can I get off of this deadbeat team and join a winning team?

Okay, that's just eight, seventeen short of twenty-five, but you get the picture. And now you may be able to picture that your total stress level is an accumulation of the anxiety caused by coping with problems instead of growing to overcome them.

Back to our thought exercise. Now, what if we spend equal time in each of the five mental states we've reviewed: Lay Blame, Justify, Shame, Obligation, and Responsibility? That means that 80 percent of the time we aren't giving ourselves credit for creating, choosing, or attracting our reality. Only in Responsibility (20 percent in our example) do we give ourselves credit for it, and that's when we make better choices, better decisions, and better commitments. Only when we take credit for creating, choosing, or attracting the bad (80 percent) can we transform it into the good.

You and I are far more powerful and able than we usually give ourselves credit for. When you're operating from Responsibility, you're living the life you choose to live, rather than a life you're willing to simply accept.

Many people ask: "What is an example of being in Responsibility?" My answer is this: All is well, and you are feeling unburdened, self-empowered, and full of options. In other words, you feel free, powerful, and at choice. You want what you have and have what you want.

Catching yourself in the mental state of Responsibility is worth noticing and celebrating, so that you can return there again and again.

> ## Responsibility Practice
>
> Where in your life, work, and relationships are you in Responsibility? To ask a different way, where in your life, work, and relationships:
>
> - is all well? or,
> - you are feeling unburdened, self-empowered, and full of options? or,
> - you want what you have and have what you want?
>
> For each that you identify, claim the win. It's a great thing. Congratulations.

Quit

There are a couple of other positions in The Responsibility Process that we haven't yet explored: Quit and Denial. Let's first look at Quit.

When you go to that valueless boring meeting out of Obligation, how easy is it to be totally checked in, present in the here and now, and authentic? Nearly impossible, right? I know, I see it all the time. Sometimes when I ask that question, clients say, "Christopher, that would be insane." The reason you can't very well be present and authentic when you are coping is that if you did get totally present, you would actually be in Responsibility and might say something like "Wow, this is a really valueless meeting. Can we do something different that will make better use of our time and move the business forward?" But at the moment, you might not be willing to have the consequences that come along with that, so instead you mentally Quit. You disengage. You put the I-can-cope-with-this-nonsense-for-ninety-minutes look on your face and then run your own home movies in your mind to pass the time.

In Quit you think you have parked the problem, but it's just on temporary hold. It will return. And it is costing you mental and emotional energy.

If you look at The Responsibility Process, you'll see that Quit is off to the side of the chart, just to the right of Shame and Obligation. As I have described The Responsibility Process so far, it is a linear stepwise process model that starts at the bottom and ends at the top (if you actually graduate from each level to the next rather than get stuck). Quit, out to the right of Shame and Obligation, introduces a new dynamic. Rather than a linear move, it is a lateral move to a way station, loop, sidetrack, or eddy connected to Shame and Obligation. You hang out there to escape the pain of Shame or Obligation.

Why do we have a temporary escape from Shame and Obligation? Again, the answer has to do with anxiety. If you think about it, in Lay Blame and Justify we vent and externalize our anxiety, which we could look at as blowing off steam. However in Shame and Obligation we're building it up internally. If we do not know how to consciously learn and grow by taking ownership of the problem and getting ourselves to the mental state of Responsibility, then perhaps we need an escape valve for our angst. Quit is the escape valve. We enter Quit when the pain of Shame or Obligation is unbearable.

Listen to this story of Quit: I once thought I could not have the job I wanted. So I never tried to get that job. But I also never let go of wanting that job. That's Quit—wanting something but thinking you can't have it. One day I chose to confront the truth—that if I never tried to get that job I'd never have it. So I tried. And I got the job, and it felt so good.

Think about people who mentally quit on their dream. Well-intentioned parents, teachers, and others tell them "that career" is way too risky and doesn't make sense. So they go to college to be a lawyer, doctor, accountant, or teacher like others say they should. And they wake up fifteen years later thinking *What the hell am I doing in this job I hate? I'm going to go chase my dream.* Or worse, they remain trapped in Quit and never wake up.

When we enter the mental state of Quit, we do not solve our problems, instead we put them in a mental parking lot hoping to pretend they aren't really problems. However, the problems will always come back.

Here's another example of how I landed in Quit. For years, fans of The Responsibility Process have been asking me to write the book on it. A few years ago I made a logical, strategic decision to write the book, except that I wasn't really ready and didn't know it. I had not yet practiced Responsibility enough myself and integrated the practices enough into my own being to be able to authentically write the book. But I'm getting ahead of myself, because I did not know that then. So like a good strategic planner, I turned the goal into some objectives and blocked out time on my calendar to write.

One Thursday at 3:00 p.m. I sat down to write in Partnerwerks headquarters in Comfort, Texas. It was on my calendar, 3:00 to 5:00 p.m.: Write the responsibility book. I placed my fingers on the keyboard, and my mind went blank. My response? I looked like a pianist getting ready to attack the keyboard, I reared back, raised my hands and fingers in the air and then lunged them down over my keyboard expecting I could force something out. Nothing. *Uh oh,* I thought, *this is a problem.* My anxiety started to rise. My cheeks flushed with embarrassment, and I felt ashamed. *I'm the expert on this stuff,* I thought, *and if anybody can write the book it's me.* Well that didn't help, because I was beating myself up pretty good about not making progress in three minutes. So then I said to myself, *Okay I don't deserve to beat myself up for being human, BUT I DO HAVE TO WRITE THIS BOOK!* Oh joy. Obligation. So I poised my fingers over the keyboard again and challenged myself to write anything, gibberish, nonsense, it just didn't matter, write. Nothing. The anxiety confronted me so much that I had to do something. So what did I do? I turned off my computer, left my office, got in my car, drove to the golf course, got out my clubs, and played golf. I thought, *Hey, give it some space to percolate in your brain and come back to it later.* Right.

Next Tuesday, 3:00 to 5:00 p.m., I had blocked out the time on my calendar to write the book. Another ten minutes in front of my computer with no idea of where to start or what to write. You guessed it. I turned the computer off and got on my bike to ride. This happened a couple of more times before I realized I was at Quit. I asked myself what the real problem was, that I could own and do something about, so that I could have what I want. The answer came. I don't really want to write the book now. Yes, I would like to have the completed book, but I don't actually see myself writing it now.

Wow, the angst lifted when that clarity came. Yes I wanted a book but I didn't want to invest the time and energy to write it just then. The realization was freeing—that's what clarity does for you. I made a new choice to return the book project to the back burner, and it felt good. I was in Responsibility again.

So I turned to Quit when I faced something hard, and rather than find the real problem and face it (we'll learn more about how to do this in the next chapter), I would escape to the golf course or putting in miles on my bike.

In Quit, we aren't authentic, present, or speaking our truth. Here are some phrases that illustrate Quit:

- "Someday I'll deal with that, but not now."

- "Whatever!"

- "If only the cards had been dealt a little differently, I'd be in my dream job."

- "Only thirteen years, four months, two weeks, and seven days until retirement."

When learning The Responsibility Process and starting their responsibility practice, for many people Quit is the most challenging of the mental states to clearly understand. They ask, "Is it wrong to quit a job? Is that Quit?"

The Responsibility Process

First, it's never wrong to be human. These mental states are not about right or wrong. Right/wrong thinking—to be morally good and do the right thing—is what got us into this predicament as a society in the first place, and it is one of the conditioned habits we want to change. When people ask that question, I offer the viewpoint that if you are quitting a job to escape a problem that will return again and again in your next job, then it might well be an action you are generating from the mental state of Quit. But if you are moving on from a job feeling complete and satisfied that you have done all you can there and you have more to give that is needed and wanted in the job or career you are moving to, then that's not Quit. That looks like freedom, power, and choice to me. In Quit you will always feel incomplete—you will have thoughts of *what if?* What if the project hadn't failed? What if my boss liked me better? What if I had spoken up earlier? What if? What if? In Responsibility you will feel complete with the past and powerful in the present.

So, let's look at how to get out of Quit. First, as you may recall, when we refuse to accept the answer our mind is handing to us in one of the coping states, we leave that state behind and graduate to the next state. So, you want to recognize the signs that you are avoiding or attempting to escape a problem that will keep returning until you deal with it. We hide in Quit because we don't know how to create the results we really want. The exit for Quit is easy to explain but often hard to master. To escape the mental state of Quit, confront it directly and with compassion. You call yourself out gently for being in Quit. You ask yourself, *What new truth or insight must I get so that I can know what I really want and have it?*

When you do this, your mind works with you to move you into Responsibility where you can think more clearly and resourcefully—and the possibilities start to flow.

Responsibility Practice

Identify one or more things in your life, work, or relationships that meet the criteria for Quit: (1) you want it, (2) you've parked the want away in your mind because you think you can't (or shouldn't) have it, and (3) it's still there and reminds you now and again that you still want it.

Consider why it never really goes away and keeps saying, "Hello, I'm still here."

Allow yourself to explore what you really really want about it and how you can have it.

What About Denial?

Denial is at the bottom of the stack of words, below Lay Blame. So why present it last? Because it's an invisible or assumed part of The Responsibility Process. Remember we said the first thing the mind does when something goes wrong is Lay Blame. That's Lay Blame, not Denial. So what's Denial doing there? It's a reminder that the reason we have a problem is probably because we were ignoring the existence of something either through choice or through limited understanding.

Like the rest of The Responsibility Process, Denial is far easier to spot in others than in ourselves. We see other people who are oblivious to a life, work, or relationship issue that we can clearly see. Maybe it's diet, exercise, sleep deprivation, damaging team habits, money issues, arrogance, verbosity, career-limiting moves, etc. We think to ourselves, *When are they going to face the truth and confront reality?* Well guess what? There is nothing wrong with them. Denial isn't wrong. Oh, our culture makes it out to be this horrible moral and ethical ignorance, as if people are in Denial because they have made a reasoned choice to avoid learning and seeing the truth. I don't think so. Denial is simply ignoring the existence of something. You could think of it as the opposite of focus, awareness, or attention.

You and I are great at ignoring the existence of things. We do it all the time. I've seen studies reporting that Denial is one of the top five reasons senior executives fail. There is something going on in their market, operating environment, or company that they are not aware of. They are ignoring the existence of it. Why? Because they are focused on other things. They just didn't see it coming.

In the field of futuring and forecasting, there is a principle that says the bullet that kills you comes from a direction you aren't looking. For that reason, organizations set up various scanning systems—like 360-degree radar—constantly scanning the operating environment for signs or clues that there are activities, trends, or something else that could hurt the organization if it doesn't pay attention.

How many times have you heard—or said—"Never saw it coming!"

Winston Churchill famously set up his own military intelligence unit to give him unvarnished details of what was happening in the field during the war. Why? He knew the chain of officers reporting to him would likely operate from the normal human condition of confirmation bias. They would hide bad news for which they could get blamed. Churchill assumed he would find himself in denial about what was really going on if he simply believed the reports of his military officers. So he set up an intelligence unit that was specifically designated to find and bring him the worst possible news.

Many companies aggressively innovate to kill their own products by finding the replacement products. They understand something about denial. They know that if you try to protect your cash cow, somebody will enter your market with its replacement. Isn't that what the market disruption game is?

So what can you do about Denial? First, be willing to completely accept the consequences of ignorance. Consciously choose your purpose, direction, and source of fulfillment in life so your work will be play and your discoveries and accomplishments will make you deliriously happy.

Then if something comes out of the blue and turns out to be a problem, so be it. That sounds very conceptual so let me give you an example. In the past four US presidential election cycles, I've listened to hundreds of smart men and women make some form of this statement: "If that guy wins, my life is ruined." And so we are clear, I heard this from people on both sides of the election about the candidate they did not want to win. I thought to myself, *Wow, I'm not willing to let any president ruin my life. I'll figure out how to adapt and thrive regardless of which way the political winds blow.* You see, I believe if I care that much about something, then I probably ought to get involved and do something about it. I don't care that much about national politics. Oh sure, I usually have a preference, and I talk with my wife about what's best for us so we don't cancel each other's votes. But I don't care enough to involve myself in the campaigns. Why? I believe I am pursuing something much more valuable for humanity than party politics. I'm mastering responsibility, making The Responsibility Process known, and supporting efforts to help others master it. So if by chance, my ignoring national politics leads to something that causes a significant problem for me, then I'll accept it as a consequence of my choices. That's what Responsibility is—the willingness to have the consequences of your choices.

Responsibility Practice

In what direction do you want to develop your awareness? And in what areas are you happy to accept the consequences of possibly ignoring the existence of something?

Summary

In this chapter you have had a thorough introduction to The Responsibility Process. Understanding how our minds process thoughts about avoiding and taking 100 percent responsibility gives us keen insight into our lives, work, and relationships. It shows us how we get stuck in mental states where we cope with problems rather than solve them for good. And it shows us that the mental state of Responsibility is available to us—always, even when we think it isn't.

We learned that The Responsibility Process is triggered by frustration or anxiety and that the source of the anxiety is the conflict between what we want and what we have.

We learned about the cause-and-effect logic in each of the mental states in The Responsibility Process. We also learned about the dynamics of moving from one mental state to another. As long as we accept the answer our mind offers us, we will remain stuck in that mental state. We exit the mental state when we refuse to accept the answer our mind offers us there. To exit Lay Blame, we refuse to blame another. To exit Justify, we refuse to believe our story. To exit Shame we decide to stop beating ourselves up. And to exit Obligation we refuse to feel trapped.

Perhaps most important, we learned that The Responsibility Process is natural. It works the same way in all of us. That means we are not wrong for blaming, justifying, beating ourselves up, or feeling trapped. We don't do those things because we are bad; we do them because we are human, and this is how humans respond to anxiety.

In the next chapter, we will look at the three keys for unlocking The Responsibility Process so that we can apply, practice, and ultimately master responsibility.

4

The Three Keys to Responsibility

Now that you know there is a predictable pattern in your mind—The Responsibility Process—processing your thoughts about taking or avoiding Responsibility, you may be wondering *What do I do about it!?* That's where the Three Keys to Responsibility come in. These three keys unlock and provide you with access to The Responsibility Process:

- Intention

- Awareness

- Confront

This chapter will get you started applying the three keys (figure 4.1) to unlock and access The Responsibility Process today. Then, after you know how to apply the basics, I'll show you how to treat the three keys as mental powers that you can develop and rely on for the rest of your life.

The Three Keys to Responsibility

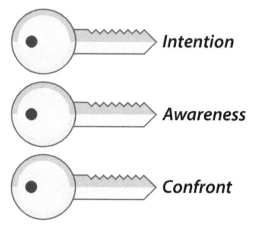

Figure 4.1. *The Three Keys to Responsibility.*

Remember, the Three Keys to Responsibility comprise the second of three tools offered in this book for understanding and practicing responsibility. The Responsibility Process, described in chapter 3 was the first tool, and you will learn about the third tool in chapter 5.

The Basics of Applying Each Key

I bet you can identify at least one upset or frustration in your life that has triggered The Responsibility Process. Why? You will get the most out of this section by applying each of the keys to an existing problem. Doing so produces valuable new degrees of freedom, choice, and power.

Just as I have capitalized words that name the mental states, I will capitalize each key, treating it as a formal name.

Key 1: The Intention to Operate from Responsibility

The first key to Responsibility is *Intention*. Specifically, it is your Intention to operate from the mental state of Responsibility when things go wrong.

Operating from any other mental state means coping with the problem rather than owning and solving it. Only in Responsibility can you release yourself from that frustration or upset. An Intention to operate from Responsibility is an intention to be resourceful and to lead yourself to freedom, choice, and power.

Intention is the first of the three keys because if you don't intend to get to the mental state of Responsibility when life presents you with your next frustration, upset, or problem, then the other two keys are irrelevant. Remember, there is a gulf of a difference between being a responsible person and taking 100 percent responsibility. Practicing Responsibility begins with the clear Intention to actually practice responsibility.

Want an example? Think of two workers, each temporarily blocked from making progress on their assignments. They each feel frustrated. The first worker has no clear Intention to operate from Responsibility. In this instance he may unconsciously (and naturally) land in the mental state of Justify, and he unconsciously (and naturally) operates from that mental state. He tells himself, *There's nothing I can do until the block clears.* So nothing is exactly what he does. The second worker thinks the same thing at first (after all, he is human and always subject to The Responsibility Process), and then he catches himself. He recalls his strong Intention to operate from Responsibility. So he asks himself, *How can I take ownership of this situation?* Soon he realizes that he can help clear the block or he could identify and fix the root cause so the block doesn't happen again. With this resourceful thinking, worker two moves forward with freedom, choice, and power to produce a result that matters.

Applying this first key Intention calls the question: Do you intend to operate from Responsibility when things go wrong? Or do you intend to operate from Lay Blame, Justify, Shame, Obligation, and Quit? It's a simple and straightforward question with profound implications. If your answer is that you intend to operate from Responsibility, then I recommend you cement that Intention with a clear commitment: "I demand to get to the mental state of Responsibility as soon as possible whenever I experience upset, frustration, anxiety, and problems in my life. I will own it." Make this feeling of ownership a deliberate Intention.

Realize this one clear Intention—to get to Responsibility—is committing to a way of being every day, day in and day out, for the rest of your life. Responsibility is not just a character trait, it's what you practice.

Responsibility Practice

Start by identifying a frustration or upset you are experiencing. Ask yourself if you are willing to address it from the mental state of Responsibility where you can resolve it and give yourself newfound freedom, choice, and power. If you answer, "Yes, I am willing," then ask yourself if you truly intend to get to the mental state of Responsibility. *Note:* You may not know *how* to get there yet (there are other keys to apply). Knowing how isn't necessary to create and hold the Intention. Intention is the *why* that precedes the *how*.

Key 2: Awareness of Your Mental State

The second key to Responsibility is *Awareness*. Specifically, it is the Awareness of your mental state in The Responsibility Process when you are dealing with an upset.

The first key Intention calls us to "intend to *operate* from Responsibility." It doesn't call us to "always stay in Responsibility." This is an important distinction. We admit that because we are human we are going to experience thoughts of Lay Blame, Justify, Shame, Obligation, and Quit. And, we also acknowledge that we don't have to act on each of those thoughts. The second key Awareness calls us to notice our mental state when we are upset or frustrated so that we can make a conscious choice about whether we operate from that mental state.

The specific practice is this: Notice—develop the Awareness of—where you are in The Responsibility Process when you are frustrated or upset. Remember, the trigger that kicks off The Responsibility Process is an upset of any size. So when you experience an upset, learn to ask yourself, *Where am I in The Responsibility Process?* Then check whether you are in Lay Blame, Justify, Shame, Obligation, or Quit.

In the example of the two workers in the previous section, the first worker was not conscious of his mental state while the second worker was. Awareness that you are in one of the mental states, plus having a strong Intention to operate from Responsibility will propel you toward the mental state of Responsibility.

Responsibility Practice

Think of an existing upset or frustration you are experiencing. Can you identify one or more of the mental states where you are hanging out around that upset? If so, you have just successfully applied the Awareness key. Congratulations. In the next section I will tell you what happens next.

As you develop Awareness of these mental states in yourself, note your thoughts, feelings, emotions, and behaviors. Get to know what it is like to be you when you are in Lay Blame, Justify, Shame, Obligation, Quit, and Responsibility. The more you get to know yourself in these mental states, the faster you will gain Awareness when you land in one. Don't criticize yourself for landing in any of these states. That's both a waste of time and energy and a way to land in Shame. Instead, practice compassion for self and be grateful for your increased ability to recognize the mental states. That's Awareness at work.

A special note: This is about your personal practice, not about calling out others. Because we judge ourselves by our good intentions and others by their behavior, it is a thousand times easier to observe The Responsibility Process in others than in ourselves. So if you observe others blaming, rather than calling them out, show some compassion. Ask yourself what Lay Blame of your own you may have been unaware of. Then celebrate your growth in Awareness.

Combining These First Two Keys

Consider how Intention plus Awareness work together beautifully for you. If you can notice that you are angry or annoyed with others, and you are thinking that they should change, then you are in the mental state of Lay Blame. Congratulations for that Awareness. Now, if your Intention to operate from Responsibility is strong enough, then you will stop blaming and graduate to Justify. That's how Intention and Awareness work together to move you through The Responsibility Process.

There is a reliable dynamic at play here. When you combine a strong Intention to operate from Responsibility with the Awareness that you are in a coping state, let's say Lay Blame for the sake of example, then you make a swift decision to stop blaming. You exit that mental state (Lay Blame) and graduate to the next one. Examples follow for each of the mental states.

If you are telling yourself stories about not having what you want due to the weather, economy, business culture, traffic, city government, your own busyness, etc., then you are stuck momentarily in Justify. Congratulations again for your Awareness. If your Intention to operate from Responsibility is strong enough, then you will stop justifying and graduate to Shame.

In Shame, you will be feeling ashamed or guilty. You might be asking, "What's wrong with me?" If so, stop. Here's an important principle about Awareness. Whatever we focus our attention on grows. So if you ask yourself, "What's wrong with me?" you will find answers! You can generate an endless list:

- "I didn't go to the right school."

- "I was born to the wrong parents."

- "I took the wrong first job."

- "I shouldn't have tried."

- and on and on.

Instead of asking "What's wrong with me?" realize that if you are beating yourself up, then you are functioning normally. And that means there is nothing wrong with you.

In Shame there are better questions to ask:

- How long do I deserve to beat myself up for being human when there is nothing wrong with me?

- What do I want (specifically related to this problem)?

So, again by combining Intention and Awareness, if you catch yourself in Shame and you have a strong Intention to operate from Responsibly, then you will stop beating yourself up and graduate to Obligation.

In Obligation you probably feel like you have to be/do/have something you don't want. Feeling trapped or burdened is a sure sign of Obligation. Recognizing it and seeing it for what it is (i.e., an unresourceful mental state) is excellent Awareness. Congratulations. If your Intention to operate from Responsibility is strong, then you will start a mental search for how you can effectively release yourself from the trap. Your mind will start looking for new insights from the mental state of Responsibility. Yay! You have used Awareness and Intention together to move through The Responsibility Process. If you can do it once, you can do it again, and again, and again.

And if you are just tired and feel like giving in and giving up, then you may be in Quit. You know what to do. Notice that you are operating from Quit when you have an Intention to operate from Responsibility. Your mind is already programed to help you graduate from Quit to Responsibility. Your mind will start an internal search for new insights and breakthroughs that will help you make new choices to have what you want.

Here is an example of how this whole sequence can unfold rapidly when your practice is strong: On a recent client trip I followed the directions I received from a car company on an earlier trip. Previously, they said,

"Just go to the kiosk at the airport, no reservation needed." The first time it worked great. This time, the kiosk was jammed, and the attendant was only serving people with a reservation. I was not happy. For a good five minutes I blamed the telephone agent from a month earlier for telling me I didn't need a reservation. Then I realized I was blaming instead of solving the problem. My next realization was justifying how much busier it was today versus the previous trip. Maybe that explains why the agent told me just to go to the kiosk THAT day. She didn't mean every day. Now I felt stupid. However I have a commitment to catch myself in Shame quickly and forgive myself for being human. So, I looked around and found a competing car company. I went over, arranged for a car, and was on my way.

In the next section, we'll learn how to apply the third key to Responsibility.

Responsibility Practice

If you have not already done so, place a visual of The Responsibility Process prominently where you will see it frequently as a reminder to practice Intention and Awareness. You can write it on your whiteboard, on a card in your wallet or purse, or on your bathroom mirror! Download a full color pdf of The Responsibility Process poster from ChristopherAvery.com in either A4 or Letter size, and in more than twenty-five languages (even Klingon).

Key 3: Confront Your Internal Conflict

The third key to Responsibility is *Confront*. Specifically, it means to Confront—or face—yourself and your upset directly, rather than cope with it, so that you can uncover the real problem behind the upset, resolve it, and grow.

Confront is a bold word. Some people are put off by it, so let's clarify. One meaning of *confront* is "to face in hostility or defiance; oppose." That's not the meaning we are using as a key to Responsibility. The other meaning is "to face." This second meaning drops the defiance toward another person. Instead it means the ability to face ourselves and our upsets so that we can examine them and get to the truth about them.[1]

Confront means to face yourself and look inward because you are the one who is upset. To free yourself from the problem, you must face and examine the perceived conflict in your mind between what you have and what you want. Once you've done that, you can discover how to resolve it so you never have that particular problem again.

Let's look at an example. Recently, I was flying for an important meeting. Midflight, the plane developed a maintenance issue. When the pilots reported it, the airline diverted the flight to a different airport hundreds of miles away from where I wanted to be. I would miss my meeting. I immediately felt quite upset. I checked my Intention and asked myself, *What do I want in this situation?* Before that moment I had wanted to arrive relaxed and on time to the meeting, but that was no longer possible. I also realized I wanted the plane to land safely, what had been an assumed Intention before now became primary. Sometimes reality changes our priorities. Then, I asked myself, *Where am I in The Responsibility Process?* I realized that I was blaming the airline. Their mechanical issue would make me miss my meeting! Finally, I applied the Confront key. I faced my upset as its owner and asked myself silently, *What belief, assumption, or expectation could I let go of to get unstuck?* That's when I realized I did not have to remain a victim. The truth is that travel delays are common. A responsible traveler can anticipate and plan for delays. Today, I almost never travel on the day of an important presentation, always leaving room for plan A and plan B to fail, leaving room for plan C and maybe plan D too. As a result, I am freer, more powerful, and always at choice when I travel—even with delays. I am a gloriously unstressed traveler.

When you practice Confront, you choose to face and fully experience your anxiety while examining, observing, and searching your thoughts for what's true that you're not seeing. When you gain experience doing this, you realize that the same anxiety that causes us to get stuck in coping states can be put to use to poke and provoke our mind in Responsibility to uncover the false expectation or assumption that we could not previously see. Remember: in the top-tier mental state of Responsibility, our complex reasoning abilities are vast compared to any of the mental states below the line.

It takes some courage to utilize the Confront key since it is more comfortable in the short term to avoid Responsibility. As you successfully practice Confront, you build confidence that you can face and own larger and larger problems, and that's when your courage grows.

Responsibility Practice

Invite yourself to face—Confront—one of your ongoing upsets or frustrations. Ask yourself what belief or assumption you might be holding on to that isn't necessarily true. Or you could ask yourself what insightful bit of truth or clarity you aren't yet seeing that could give you a new perspective and allow you to generate new and truly freeing choices about how to respond.

Developing the Keys for Self-Leadership

Successful entrepreneur and mentor to entrepreneurs Zach Nies tells me I'm teaching The Responsibility Process and the Three Keys to Responsibility in reverse order. Zach prefers to teach the three keys as the keys to self-leadership—to lead yourself, take ownership of and accomplish anything:

- **Intention** is the stuff of setting meaningful targets and being pulled toward them.

- **Awareness** is the first step toward change and how leaders grow in understanding themselves and others.

- **Confront** is facing progressively larger challenges in order to grow as a leader.

After teaching the three keys, Zach then describes The Responsibility Process as "your brain in failure mode."

I think Zach has a point. Let's dive deeper into the dynamics of the three keys to see how you can hone your mental powers of Intention, Awareness, and Confront to lead yourself and others to freedom, choice, and power while producing results that matter.

As powers of the mind that you were born with, and that you can choose to exercise consciously or not, these three keys are natural. You are already equipped to put them to use. More importantly, the three keys comprise a system dynamic such that when you develop one, it draws on the other two. So if you set a very high Intention, it certainly challenges your Awareness and invites you to Confront fears and uncertainties. When you develop Awareness of a new truth, it Confronts other related beliefs and assumptions and invites you to raise your Intention in those areas. Think of the three keys as dynamic, as an iterative and adaptive mental system for lifelong growth and self-leadership.

When you look at the keys this way—as a system dynamic for self-leadership—you see that there is an advanced application of the keys to augment the basic application with which we opened the chapter. Instead of the discrete, problem-by-problem application of Intention, Awareness, and Confront described at the beginning of this chapter, the advanced application views the keys as mental capabilities that you can develop and hone over time. You can view your powers of Intention, Awareness, and Confront as an ever-expanding flow of personal power to lead yourself to the life, relationships, and work of your dreams.

In the remaining sections of this chapter, we examine each key briefly as a life skill that you can hone and develop through practice and application. They can become daily tools with which you address life. And as you use them, these mental powers become stronger and stronger.

Responsibility Practice

Since the keys to Responsibility are also mental powers you can develop for self-leadership, consider how you will use your powers of Intention, Awareness, and Confront to lead yourself, and possibly others, to freedom, choice, and power while producing results that matter.

Honing Your Intention—The Winning Key

Intention is defined as "the thing that you plan to do or achieve: an aim or purpose."[2] For example, "I intend to meet with my team today." It is a determination to feel, behave, or experience something in a certain way. I've heard Intention described as a stretching or bending of the mind toward some object or outcome. Intention is also described as a fixedness of attention, as in to focus or concentrate. It's a sense of earnestness and impulse toward something. I've even heard it called an internal carrier wave.

Let me illustrate with a simple story. The first house Amy and I owned was in a lovely and hilly neighborhood in Austin, Texas, called Northwest Hills. The house sat at the bottom of not one hill, but two. Although the landscape was lush and green, it was also humid and stuffy, and our views were into the hillsides comprising the neighbors' yards and tree trunks. A few years later as our family grew and we started thinking of moving, I remember looking at a house sitting high on a hill with a beautiful view. I could also feel a breeze there that would not be felt at our house a few blocks away at the bottom of those hills. I remember thinking *I want to live at the top of a hill with a view.* It was the type of *I want this!* thought that sticks. I'm sure you know what I mean. As we looked at properties, being on a hill with a view became one of the criteria. You won't be surprised that our next house was high on a hill in Austin with expansive views in three points of the compass. And today our house in Comfort, Texas, sits on the edge of a hill almost 300 feet above the Guadalupe River and looks out over the river valley more than five miles to hills on the other side.

Thus, about twenty years ago I generated a simple thought, an Intention, to live high on a hill with a view. And for nineteen years, that Intention has been met. And that feels good.

There is nothing unique about this story. The Intention to live on a hill is one of thousands, or perhaps millions, of intentions I've generated. It's not the most important nor largest of my intentions. Nor did it require significant effort or time to realize. And most importantly, there is nothing unique about me for having and realizing intentions because we all do it. It simply illustrates what an Intention is: the thing you plan to do or achieve; a determination to feel, behave, or experience something; a stretching or bending of the mind toward some object or outcome; a fixedness of attention; a sense of earnestness and impulse toward something; an internal carrier wave.

Intention is an essential component of free will, your individual ability to decide what you want to experience. It's a fundamental aspect of being human. If we look at synonyms for Intention it's easy to see how much we apply Intention in business. We have visions and purposes, we develop strategies and plans, and we set goals and objectives. They all mean something we aim to make true, something we pursue and intend to accomplish or attain.

Responsibility Practice

Think of some of the intentions you have generated in your life that came true or are in the process of being realized. They don't have to be examples of massive things, nor of intentions that required great effort, fortitude, or time. Simply think of things in your life where you thought to yourself *I want to do, be, or experience X* and then you did.

When you recall intentions that you set and then met, how does it feel?

Feeling the Win

I call Intention the winning key. When you consciously set intentions and meet them, you feel like you are winning.

The Responsibility Process shows us that if we are experiencing what we intend—or want—to experience, then we feel free rather than trapped, we feel powerful rather than powerless, and we feel in a position of choice (what I call "at choice") rather than in a position of effect ("at effect" or "no choice"). Life is good.

When we have what we want, we are winning. When we feel blocked and stopped from having what we want, then we get anxious, frustrated, and upset—and then The Responsibility Process kicks in and the coping patterns start. For this reason, understanding and developing your mental powers of Intention is key to practicing and eventually mastering Responsibility.

So, how can you develop your power of Intention?

In the next section I introduce a practice you can start right now. I offer many more in part III, "Practicing and Mastering Responsibility." Engage in these practices and you will rapidly strengthen your power of Intention and your ability to win in life, work, and relationships.

Responsibility Practice

Are you experiencing day by day the life, work, and relationships that you truly intend? If so, claim the win. Or, is your day-to-day reality falling short of what you truly want to experience in life, work, and relationships? Simply notice and know that you have the capability to develop and hone your powers of Intention.

Discover What You Want

Two primary approaches exist to develop your Intention. Intending to operate from Responsibility is the first, as described at the beginning of this chapter. The second is actively discovering what you truly want in your life, believing it can be so, aligning to it, and noticing and claiming the win when intentions come true.

If you think this sounds trivial, or maybe even self-centered, I assure you it isn't. Every bit of upset or anxiety we experience is a sign that we are feeling blocked from having something we want. Maybe it is a happier life, a better job, or a special relationship. Or maybe it is just to get to the meeting without wearing our coffee. It could be anything, large or small. Consciously—intentionally—uncovering what that is and operating from Responsibility to get unstuck, will provide the breakthrough growth, time and again, to live the life of your dreams.

Later in the book, after you have seen the three tools (The Responsibility Process, the three Keys to Responsibility, and the Catch Sooner Game in chapter 5), then we'll explore Intention more deeply. In chapter 6, "Lead Yourself First," I'll give you a practice for discovering and pursuing your deepest intentions—a sort of life GPS or guidance system—as well as a daily practice you can use by yourself and with your teams to develop Intention and ensure you are winning.

Responsibility Practice

One of my students says, "Knowing what you want is the hard part." That can be true for many of us especially if, like me, you grew up being told what you *should* want (which is a surefire way to invalidate your powers of Intention). We may have developed a counter-intention: *Don't allow yourself to want (because you'll get in trouble, or because you can't have it)*. So for us, the first exercise is to allow ourselves to want again. How? Practice. Spend five minutes every day for a week writing down your wants large or small. Do it privately and don't edit or judge. Let it all come out. Each line of the list starts with "I want . . ."

Note: This isn't just about material things you may want. You likely also have moments, settings, and relationships you want to experience as well—who you want to be and what you want to do. The seeds of these wants already exist inside of you. Let them out.

If you want some help with this, watch the 2007 movie *The Bucket List* about two aging men (played by Jack Nicholson and Morgan Freeman) dying from cancer who make a list of experiences they intend to have before dying.[3]

And if "I want . . ." is too wide open and you want a little more structure, then an incremental step toward that is to write "I prefer A to B." Here are some examples:

- I prefer Comfort, Texas, to Regina, Saskatchewan.
- I prefer living at the top of a hill to living at the bottom.
- I prefer entrepreneurship to employment.

Honing Your Awareness—The Change Key

Awareness is the change key because as we become aware of facts, points of view, and our own thoughts, we are able to change in the direction of our desires. Without new Awareness, we may not know that change is available or possible.

Awareness as a mental power is about knowing ourselves by observing ourselves while also trying on new perspectives and viewpoints. The French-born author Anaïs Nin wrote, "We don't see things as they are; we see them as we are."[4] She was referencing two women who had different opinions of The Seine. Nin's quote observes that the women's views of the river revealed more about them than about the river. Our viewpoint determines what we perceive. When we change our point of view, we change what we perceive. The mental states in The Responsibility Process demonstrate this. You are now aware that you perceive a problem quite differently from the position of Lay Blame than you do from Responsibility.

In my doctoral program, I studied with the management scholar Karl Weick. He tells a story of three Major League baseball umpires disagreeing about how they each call balls and strikes: "The first one said, 'I calls them as they is.' The second one said, 'I calls them as I sees them.' The third and cleverest umpire said, 'They ain't nothin' till I calls them.'"[5] Weick thought the third umpire was wise in that only he realized his own unconscious biases were constructing his perception of a ball and a strike, especially when they were close calls. This is a type of Awareness I see in people who practice responsibility. They realize that they are constructing their own perceptions of reality, good or bad (a theme we've visited before), and that allows them to be less critical of themselves and others and more open to observing themselves without judgment, so that they can learn and change.

Do you know what the number-one approach to formal leadership development is? Developing self-awareness is the top approach, and it has been for as long as there has been a leadership development industry. Why? Leadership is a relationship issue. If you lack Awareness of self—of your preferences, biases, and how you are perceived—how can you expect others to believe in you, to trust you, and to invite you to lead them?

Leadership is also about pursuing change. You are probably aware of the quote "The first step toward change is awareness."[6] Developing your Awareness means to examine and expand your consciousness to understand alternative perspectives and to find and let go of limiting beliefs, false assumptions, unreal expectations, and judgmental viewpoints. This will allow you to see reality more clearly instead of how your well-intentioned shapers—society, parents, teachers, relatives, employers—would have you see it.

The famous change quote by Nathaniel Branden, "The first step toward change is awareness," has a less well-known second sentence: "The second step is acceptance." This is a keen insight. What Branden was referring to is how powerfully humans defend our judgments and expectations of reality even when those expectations are baseless. Think of a child caught in a lie who continues to defend and build on the lie, digging a deeper hole for himself, even after the lie is exposed. You and I do the same thing, if not quite as outlandishly as the child. We grumble about the traffic even when we cannot and will not do anything to change it. We don't say, "Darn gravity!" when we drop things or they roll off the table. We accept that gravity exists and that we aren't going to change it. In the same way, we *could* accept that traffic exists and let go of our frustration while we're stuck in it.

In the mental states below Responsibility—Lay Blame, Justify, Shame, Obligation, and Quit—we resist seeing things as they are. We are not as aware as we could be. In the mental state of Responsibility, we see more clearly and can accept things as they are, and that makes us more powerful.

Myriad approaches exist for expanding your consciousness for greater Awareness: Meditation, yoga, breath work, personality assessments, martial arts, psychoanalysis, 360-degree feedback, journaling, watching video of yourself presenting, life coaching, acting and improvisation classes, vocal awareness training, leadership development, the arts, and so many more. All of these can be used to introduce you to new understandings about yourself and others.

Responsibility Practice

Could we cause our own problems without being aware of it? Of course we can. Many times in my life a coach has exclaimed, "Oh Christopher, what a perfect problem for you!" What they were implying was that the root cause of my suffering was an unexamined point of view, judgment, limiting belief, or false expectation that I was holding on to. They could see it, but I could not. I lacked Awareness of my own conditioning, my own judgment. Once I became aware of that viewpoint, I changed. I could choose to modify it or let it go. Hence it was a perfect problem to support my growth. The famous biblical reference for this is in both Matthew and Luke: "Why do you look at the speck that is in your brother's eye, but do not notice the log that is in your own eye?"[7]

To develop your Awareness, intend to become aware of problems that represent a perfect problem for you. *Hint:* If the problem recurs over and over and it seems like you are constantly suffering, it might be a perfect problem. You might even ask trusted friends for their observations. Frequently we have blind spots that others can see and help us see.

Honing Your Confront—The Growth Key

Confront is the growth key because only when we Confront the real problem can we solve it. And the process of solving it expands our ability to function as a human being. It provides newfound degrees of freedom, choice, and power that we did not have before and will always have into the future. Our ability to handle reality expands. We prove over and over that we can be bigger than any problem.

How can you put Confront into practice? The best way I know is to feel yourself getting upset about something and at that moment make a conscious choice to remain present and centered while examining the upset in your mind to determine what's true about the conflict between what you have and what you want. This ability to be present, to be mindful, and to be in the moment has substantial history. It is a key element in Buddhism, Taoism, yoga, and Native-American traditions. It's why Thoreau went to Walden Pond, and it's the subject of essays and poems by Whitman and Emerson.[8]

So if we are not being present in the moment, where are we? Well, we *are* there physically, however *being present* does not mean physically there. It means mentally and emotionally available and present in the moment. If we aren't mentally present where are we? Well, due to our anxieties, we are mentally time traveling either to the past or to the future. If our anxiety takes us to the past, then we replay the event for which we are blaming another person, or justifying the conditions, shaming ourselves, or resenting a commitment we made. If our anxiety takes us to the future, then we make up our own movies about a scary problem scenario (like getting fired) that hasn't yet occurred and may never occur. You and I—as smart, ambitious, well-educated citizens—allow our upsets to send us time traveling through much of our day.

Yet, the only point of mental power is in the present, the here and now, this moment. That is why we want to develop our power to Confront problems.

Effective self-direction and leadership can be thought of as the ability to keep your head when all around you are losing theirs. This popular—and I think true—quality of leadership is taken from the opening lines of "If" by Rudyard Kipling, a poem about moral courage and about the power of utilizing Confront. Kipling writes, "If you can keep your head when all about you are losing theirs and blaming it on you . . . Yours is the Earth and everything that's in it, and—which is more—you'll be a Man, my son!"[9]

Now let's look at what it means to stay present in the face of drama and anxiety. Longtime student of The Responsibility Process and accredited coach in The Leadership Gift Program, Ashley Johnson, called me one day to report a win. He said, "Christopher, something happened yesterday that you predicted would happen one day in my responsibility practice." Ashley went on, "Yesterday I walked into a room and could feel anger in the air even though other people's backs were to me. When one of them saw me, he came over to me and began unloading on me. He was very upset about something he incorrectly assumed I had done. For the first time ever in a situation like this, I found myself at ease and centered, with no need to resist, react, defend myself, or mirror his anger. I recognized he was so upset that my attempting to correct the misunderstanding at that moment would simply escalate the problem. I felt compassion and empathy for him and realized I was exhibiting the ability to face, to Confront, and stay totally present. I actually remember thinking that even though I was being chewed out and blamed for another person's bad day, I could still continue having a perfectly wonderful day myself. And I was able to empathize with him, listen, and absorb what he was trying to say. We soon resolved the issue—likely far faster than if I'd attempted to argue or defend myself."[10]

This ability to be present in the here and now in the face of drama and anxiety adds another dimension to Confront. It is the ability to face the upset and allow it to be in your presence without you mirroring the anxiety, which means you can see it clearly and remain free, powerful, and at choice in how you respond. In this case, you have developed your power of Confront to the point where you can have drama and upsets around you without becoming judgmental, defensive, or reactive.

Recently I was on a flight with a crying baby a couple of rows behind me. While some people—including the stranger sitting next to me—were acting judgmental about the baby, its parents, or the airline that sold it a ticket for that seat, I realized the truth of the situation: *Babies fly, babies cry, I fly, I get to be present with whatever is happening. I can choose to be annoyed, or I can choose to have a perfectly magnificent day.* I took a moment to consciously empathize with the crying baby, her anxious caretakers trying to calm her, even the fellow next to me getting extremely annoyed, and all the other fellow passengers with their various judgments, evaluations, and frustrations. I silently sent my prayers of compassion to all of them, wishing them understanding and the freedom, choice, and power it brings. And I decided I could have this situation—I could face it, Confront it, be present with it—and continue to have a perfectly joyous day. It doesn't end there. Rather than intensifying in my ears, the baby's cries faded into the background. When the guy next to me saw from my compassionate smile that I wasn't going to join him in his commiseration, he settled down too.

Have the courage and wisdom to keep your head and to compassionately be with others when they are losing theirs. This is self-direction and leadership in the face of drama. It is how we can own life's negatives and transform them into positives.

Responsibility Practice

Here is how you can practice Confront to be fully present with the upset. Next time you are with someone who is anxious or upset or even perhaps hurting or ill, choose to remain fully present, empathizing, and feeling compassion for their human frailness rather than being critical, judgmental, or upset with them. Every time you do it, mark it, and claim the win for yourself.

Comfort Zone

You can think of Confront as crossing outside of our comfort zone for the sake of getting rid of an upset, and in the process, we grow. The comfort zone is a popular concept to help us think about stretching ourselves so that we can grow. You are probably familiar with the comfort zone. If you draw a circle and label the interior of that circle "my comfort zone," then you have divided your reality into two zones. Your current capabilities and areas where you have trust in yourself lie inside your comfort zone. Unfortunately the frustrations and upsets with which you are coping are in there too. Yes, it is true, if not fun to admit, that the reason we cope with these problems is that we have learned to be comfortable enough with them. I hope this doesn't mess up your concept of the comfort zone!

A host of other things lie outside of your comfort zone:

- What you want that you don't have

- Getting rid of what you have that you don't want

- Change, growth, and other newfound degrees of freedom, choice, and power

- Desired new capabilities

As noted earlier in this chapter, the "c" in Confront can also stand for courage because our ego doesn't like to be challenged and we are often humbled by what we learn about ourselves when we approach the edges of our comfort zone. Good news! The Responsibility Process and its three keys will help you incrementally manage the process of expanding your comfort zone, which builds your confidence and courage. As you do this, you also build your ability to Confront. Practicing Responsibility is a virtuous cycle.

Up to now I've made it sound like everything about Confront has to do with facing the big bad bogeyman in your head. I once believed that but no longer do. Often it is simply about uncertainty. Listen to this example. My office is in a small converted pool cabana on our property. The cabana has glass doors across the side facing the pool. And these doors face west. The afternoon sun beaming through those windows is unbearable for about six months of the year, so we installed an electric roll-out awning. Fast-forwarding a few years, one day the awning got caught in a wind gust that snapped one of the aluminum joints and slightly bent one of the aluminum arms that holds the awning up when it unrolls. I took the awning down, laid it on the pool deck, and spent some time looking for replacement parts. The manufacturer had gone out of business, and I could not find replacement parts.

I did not want to throw the awning away, but I did not know what to do to fix it, so it laid there. Last year during spring-cleaning my wife kindly asked if I would get the trash off the deck. "Trash!?" I rebutted, "That's my awning!" But I got her point. So once again I scoured the Internet looking for parts and found none. Finally out of desperation, I grabbed a couple of wrenches to remove the broken joint piece. When I removed the bolts, this one inch by two inch elbow joint that acted as a hinge fell into two pieces. The force of the wind had sheared it in two, but other than being shorn in two it did not look like it was twisted or distorted. And it looked to me as if it was cast aluminum. So I called my brother, an engineering executive for a machine shop and asked if cast aluminum can be welded. "Of course," he said, "find a TIG welder there in Comfort." Well I know welders in Comfort, but I've never known them to work on aluminum, so at lunch I stopped with the broken part and asked if they did TIG welding. "Sure" said Gary the welder. "Leave it with me and stop back after lunch." After lunch, the part looked good as new, Gary charged me $5, and I was able to reassemble the awning.

Now, here is the lesson about Confront. Was this a big angst-inducing problem that was scary for me to face? No. Was it a fairly harmless matter of uncertainty? Yes. Okay, so when I finally truly faced it, with wrench in hand, how long did it take me to completely resolve the problem? That's right, just a few hours and $5. Next question: How long did I spend not facing the problem (and not growing)? About three years.

The valuable lesson here is that learning follows—and seldom precedes—Confront. However, we were taught that we can learn first (i.e., acquire knowledge) and then skillfully apply it. Confront teaches us that's seldom true. Only when we apply ourselves to a problem can we then learn. Marshall Thurber, whom I refer to as the grandfather of this research on The Responsibility Process, says, "Learning happens in no time. It's *not* learning that takes time."[11] What Thurber means is that my three years of avoiding facing the problem kept me from learning. Then, I finally learned everything I needed to know to solve the problem in less than an hour. Yes, learning happens in no time.

Responsibility Practice

How many projects like my awning do you have lying around while you are not learning? Confront one by truly facing it and see how quickly you learn.

Summary

This was the second of three chapters each offering one of three tools for understanding and practicing responsibility. This chapter focused on the Three Keys to Responsibility: Intention, Awareness, and Confront. These three keys allow you to unlock and access The Responsibility Process so that you can produce greater freedom, power, and choice while producing results that matter.

We started with the basics of applying each key to help you move through The Responsibility Process for any given problem:

- The **Intention** to get to Responsibility for any upset so that you can resolve it,

- The **Awareness** of your mental state so that you can move off of it toward Responsibility, and

- The ability to **Confront** your internal conflict so that you can generate insights and newfound clarity that allow you to grow and overcome the problem.

We also looked at how the keys work together to move you through The Responsibility Process.

The remainder of the chapter looked at the keys as mental powers you can hone and apply for self-leadership. Intention is about discovering and pursuing what you truly want so that you can take Responsibility more naturally. Awareness is about knowing yourself in relation to others while gaining perspectives and viewpoints that help you know and align with truth, also making it more natural to take Responsibility. Confront is about your ability to stay present and centered in the face of anxiety and drama, either yours or another person's, so that you can have and handle the situation effectively rather than cope or mentally time travel.

Intention, Awareness, and Confront will be discussed again throughout the remaining chapters of this book.

5

The Catch Sooner Game

Have you tried, failed, and given up on changing one or more of your habitual thought patterns or behaviors? If so, you would not be alone. I have good news. Some—not all, but a critical piece—of what you have been taught about how to change your habits is flawed. The Catch Sooner Game corrects that easily and simply. In this chapter, I'll introduce it to you and help you start playing the Catch Sooner Game.

What is Catch Sooner? It is a four-step adaptive process for changing anything about yourself that you want to change, whether a bad habit, a vice, or a propensity to get stuck in Lay Blame or any of the other positions of The Responsibility Process. Like The Responsibility Process and the Three Keys to Responsibility, Catch Sooner is a straightforward framework that reflects how your mind naturally works (which is why Catch Sooner works). Once you learn it, you will have it with you as a tool for the rest of your life.

I've used Catch Sooner to become a nonsmoker, eat a healthy diet, turn a host of poor life and business choices and practices into a set of very effective life and business choices and practices, and more. As with the previous tools—The Responsibility Process and the Three Keys to Responsibility—I want to briefly introduce you to the tool, then in the next chapter we can apply all three tools to life, work, and relationships.

Here are the steps to the Catch Sooner Game:

1. **Catch:** Catch yourself engaging in the behavior you want to change.

2. **Change:** Demonstrate the desired behavior.

3. **Forgive:** Forgive yourself for being human and not changing faster due to unconscious programming or conditioning.

4. **Vow:** Vow to catch yourself sooner next time.

The Catch Sooner Game

Figure 5.1. *The Catch Sooner Game.*

Start back at step 1 and repeat.

What makes this change system (figure 5.1) so effective is that it employs Intention, Awareness, and Confront in a humanizing way so you don't have to feel ashamed of trying and failing. Additionally, it's effective because each step is a small, practical, immediate action that you take in the moment, so habit change becomes incremental, targeted, adaptive, and the process is iterative. Each time you catch yourself is an Intention met—a win. As you accumulate wins, the habit changes.

Responsibility Practice

What habitual thought pattern or behavior would you like to change? You may have several. Choose at least one to have in mind as you read this chapter.

Catch

Let's say you want to improve your listening skills in a meeting, and specifically, you have a habit of interrupting others that you want to break. You know that as a leader, when you interrupt others you send subtle cues that you value your voice more than you value their voice. You know it is not respectful. You don't want to be like that. You figure there may be something deeper in your consciousness that needs to change for you to feel more whole and integrated in such meetings. And you think the Catch Sooner Game can help you.

In the Catch Sooner game, your first Intention is to catch yourself sooner and sooner doing whatever it is you want to change, in this case, catching yourself in the process of interrupting someone. We know the game works so that, over days or weeks (or longer for very deeply conditioned habits), you will catch yourself earlier in the cycle of cognition and action. (Experts describe Awareness as the ability to observe your thoughts without judgment.) Once you are able to catch the thought while it is still an impulse instead of an action, then your outward behavior has changed. People will experience you differently, and you will produce different results. At that point you still have the impulse, so you will want to continue catching yourself earlier and earlier and earlier.

When you apply this to the stages in The Responsibility Process, what you come to realize is that it is okay to have the thought of Lay Blame because you are human, and humans operate from Lay Blame first when things go wrong. The important thing though is whether you act on that thought or get off of it. It is natural for all humans to trigger The Responsibility Process when things go wrong, so it is natural to have thoughts of blame.

Okay, so you have caught yourself interrupting. Good. Intention met. Congratulations.

Responsibility Practice

Consider how it can be a win to catch yourself engaging in a pattern of thought or behavior that you want to change. Next time you catch yourself engaging in a behavior you want to change, claim the win of catching rather than chastising yourself for still exhibiting the behavior.

Change

The second step is to change from the former behavior to the new behavior. So in the case of interrupting, you might switch to listening. You may even say to the other person, "Excuse me, I caught myself interrupting you when I really want to be listening. I apologize. Please continue."

The moment you catch yourself, stop the thought or behavior that you do not want. This is powerful. We are tempted to let ourselves go, telling ourselves we can push the restart button tomorrow. For instance if my Intention was to replace donuts in my diet with a healthy alternative, and I caught myself taking a bite of a donut, I would be tempted to think, *Well, I might as well finish what I started.* (That's Justify by the way.) Simply stop so that you align as rapidly as possible with your intended behavior.

I have caught myself midbite many times at a party or in a catered business meeting. Yes, I succumbed at first, and then I caught myself and I changed. I have many memories of casually walking to the waste can and dropping the unfinished delectable in. Here is the long-term result. When I travel, and I travel frequently, I eat only what I want to eat. Others say, "It is so hard to maintain a normal diet when you travel." I say, "Unless you know what you want and how to find it wherever you are in the world."

Using our interrupting example, if you catch yourself in mid-interruption simply stop. If you catch yourself an hour after the interruption, that's okay too, just note that you caught yourself. In this example, the change may be to apologize and make amends, which would follow naturally given your Intention to be a better listener and take responsibility for interrupting.

For my impulsive eating example, after I drop the high fat, high sugar thing in the trash, I head to the veggie tray, or to a nice glass of sparkling water with lemon, reinforcing the behavior I want.

The catch-change two-step sets up the natural pattern for change to be gradual rather than sudden. You are *changing* instead of wrestling with *a change*. It's a verb, changing, rather than a noun, change. Making the big sudden change is hard because it doesn't happen immediately so we experience resistance, setbacks, and failures—all deemed bad. But changing is easy when you do it bit by bit in an easy, applied, practical, and incremental way. I did not quit smoking "cold turkey." I did it gradually with a dramatic reduction at first and then a long trending down with only an occasional smoke now and then. At first it was once or twice a day, then a week, then a month, and then a year. I never quit but simply allowed myself to let it go. I'm still not technically a pure "nonsmoker" but by health, medical, and insurance standards I am.

Responsibility Practice

For one or more of the desired changes you listed earlier in this chapter, envision yourself catching yourself midact and then changing to your desired pattern.

Forgive

To forgive is the critical difference maker in this change system. After you catch yourself and change that incident, immediately forgive yourself. Let it go. Why? The sooner you accept that you are human and full of unconscious programming, the faster you will change. You are forgiving yourself for being fully, beautifully, and errantly human. Forgiveness is a powerful force for change.

Think about it. Most advice about changing our behavior is accompanied with a step to hold yourself to account. Beat yourself up. In the science of behavior modification, it is called extinguishing the unwanted behavior by punishing yourself for falling short of your expectations of self. We call that Shame. And Shame means coping with feelings of lack and of not being good enough. Yet we know from The Responsibility Process that we *are* good enough, which means that the longer we hang out in Shame, the more we reinforce old habits instead of changing them. Resistance means you get to keep the problem. Beating ourselves up for not changing is a sure way to continue not changing.

Instead, forgive yourself for being human. Accept it. Remember, Awareness is the first step to change, and acceptance is the second. Smile compassionately at allowing your old programming to show up. Let it go. This is a much faster way to change than to punish yourself for not being superhuman.

There is a Catch Sooner Game I play with all my clients. When I catch them beating themselves up for not changing, I ask them how long they deserve to beat themselves up for being human. They usually reflect for a moment, smile, forgive themselves, and brighten up immediately. Many find this one principle—compassion for self—life altering.

Responsibility Practice

For one of the habits you listed earlier, add the compassion for self—forgiving yourself and letting it go—to your mental imagery of catching and changing. Envision it repeatedly, so perhaps it will be there when it's needed.

Vow

You make promises to yourself all the time. Some of them are more effective than others, because some of them are more natural—in terms of how your mind works—than others. In the Catch Sooner Game, the promise, or vow, that you make to yourself is to catch yourself sooner the next time you trigger the habit you want to change. Having experimented with this for decades, I can vouch for its effectiveness. It is an application of Intention, Awareness, and Confront. You intend to listen more and interrupt less. With each round of Catch Sooner, you become more and more aware of your impulses, your cognitions, your assumptions, beliefs, values, etc. And with each round of Catch Sooner, you Confront all your mental programming and invite yourself to be more present the next time so that you can catch it earlier.

Catch Sooner is a gentle and effective approach to learning and unlearning, change, and growth. And there are thousands of applications of it. In fact the journey from first learning The Responsibility Process and the three keys to applying it as a novice, and then practicing as a practitioner, all the way to mastery, is a process of Catch Sooner, thousands and thousands of times. In the next section, I'll give you a specific application of Catch Sooner that you can put to work immediately.

Responsibility Practice

For one of the changes that you want to make, vow now to catch yourself next time as soon as possible so that you can start the change process.

The Daily Scorecard Game

Here is a specific application of Catch Sooner that can support you in rapidly altering your mindset so that you can spend less and less time in the coping states, and more time in Responsibility. Hundreds of people have played this game and reported astounding results. A common report I receive from people is "the Daily Scorecard Game drastically changed my Awareness and behavior in just one week."

Here's how it works. Choose one of the mental states in The Responsibility Process to focus on today. Create a scorecard that you can keep with you all day and access easily. It could be an index card that you keep in your pocket or a sticky note attached to your tablet, phone, purse, or portfolio. It could also be a note on a smart device. To create the scorecard, choose the one mental state that you want to track today. Let's say it is Lay Blame. Write "Lay Blame" at the top of the card. Then, under "Lay Blame" divide the card into two columns. Label the left column "Caught it and got off it" or, for short, just "Caught it." Label the right column "It got out." Now you have the scorecard set up and are ready to play.

The game is to catch, change, forgive, and vow to catch sooner your thoughts or actions of Lay Blame as you go through your day. When you catch yourself having a thought of Lay Blame and you get off of it before operating from that mental position, give yourself a mark, a score, in the left column. If the thought turns into action before you catch it (i.e., you do or say something blamey before you catch it) give yourself a mark for a score in the right column. Do this all day long, building greater and greater Intention, Awareness, and Confront around this one mental state as you go.

Here's how to score. At the end of the day count up all the marks in the left "Caught it" column and multiply the original number by ten. If you caught it twenty times, you would have 200 points on the Caught it side. Then count up all the marks in the right "It got out" column and multiply the original number by one. If it got out twenty times, then you would have 20 points in the right column. Total the two columns for 220 points.

Some people are confused about why you would get any points at all for laying blame on others. Your points are not for laying blame, but for the Awareness that you did. So you get points, in fact one-tenth of the points that you would get for catching it before it gets out—which is the goal after all.

To continue the game, the next day choose another of the mental states, maybe Justify, then repeat all the steps of the game. Do a different mental state each day for a week. Should you do Responsibility? Well, sure, but then it's not a change game but a celebration game, so there are no columns and a thousand points every time you catch yourself owning your power and ability to create, choose, and attract; every time you catch yourself having what you want and wanting what you have; every time you catch yourself 100 percent willing to have the consequences of your actions; and every time you feel free, powerful, and at choice.

Responsibility Practice

Which of The Responsibility Process mental states give you the greatest personal challenge? When you know which mindsets you struggle with the most, you can learn to catch them sooner and exit them faster. Therefore, it's wise to focus your energy on the mindset that gives you the biggest problem. You'll quickly see the greatest reward.

Summary

In this chapter, we learned a useful pattern that you can use to change unwanted habits and behaviors into desired habits and behaviors. We call it Catch Sooner, and it has four steps that repeat: Catch, Change, Forgive, Vow, repeat. Perhaps the most surprising element of Catch Sooner is the idea that forgiving ourselves is a faster path to changing our habits and beliefs than is beating ourselves up.

We also learned a specific application of Catch Sooner that we call the Daily Scorecard Game. You can use it to rapidly develop your Awareness of any habit.

This is also the end of part II of this book, in which we learned three powerful tools for mastering responsibility: The Responsibility Process, the Three Keys to Responsibility, and the Catch Sooner Game. The Responsibility Process describes the mind's natural pattern for processing thoughts about taking or avoiding responsibility when things go wrong. The Three Keys to Responsibility—Intention, Awareness, and Confront—are mental powers that we are each born with and that we can hone and develop for personal leadership. And the Catch Sooner Game helps us bring it all together to make the specific changes we want to make in our lives.

Now it is time to start practicing and mastering responsibility, which is the theme of part III of this book.

Part III
Practicing and Mastering Responsibility

6

Lead Yourself First

If you are looking for things to change, consider this. You can't lead or mentor others responsibly if you aren't leading yourself. Our ability to lead, teach, coach, parent, or mentor others in Responsibility depends entirely on how effectively we have integrated the practice of Responsibility into our own life.

This chapter offers some of the top breakthroughs we've seen many people face in their own responsibility practice.

The Responsibility Process Works Only When Self-Applied

It is a thousand times easier to see The Responsibility Process at work in others than in ourselves. Remember this. It is one of the most important principles for practicing responsibility.

Most people, when introduced to The Responsibility Process, start applying it to others in their life and focusing on how others should change. They ask questions like "How can I get my spouse to stop blaming?" or "How can I get my employees to take responsibility?" If you are thinking something like this about your partner, friends, coworkers, boss, direct reports, and so on, then join the crowd; you are normal.

The Responsibility Process is a tool for self-leadership. Applying it to other people will never solve the real problem or bring you increased abilities or freedoms. Only self-applying will increase your degrees of freedom, choice, and power. In the following chapters, we look at how to lead and coach others to find their freedom. Right now, you might do more harm than good by intervening, so let's focus on you first.

Responsibility Practice

Commit to applying The Responsibility Process only to yourself. Catch yourself applying it to others. Change from judgment to compassion, realizing that they are doing the best they can with what they know in the moment and that there is nothing wrong with them. Forgive yourself. Vow to catch yourself sooner next time.

Wake Up! The Cultural Trance Is Exposed

Our society treats personal responsibility as a moral imperative—as in being good or bad, right or wrong, or doing what you should or should not. We say to each other: "You should take responsibility," which means "You should be good and do as I expect." But we now know that Responsibility is more than a moral imperative. It is the mind's framework for growing or not growing.

So, do you want to succumb to the cultural trance and be normal, even though the norm is so mediocre, so controlling, and so riddled with angst and unhappiness? Or are you instead willing to explore this new awareness, this gap between what you have grown up believing and what The Responsibility Process offers? If you choose the latter, and I hope you do, then remember, "responsibility" no longer describes just your character. It describes your daily practice of freedom, choice, and power, and you get to practice every day, because the conditioning of the cultural trance is deep.

Responsibility Practice

Where in your life, work, and relationships are you being good and doing as expected, even though it's not feeling free, powerful, or at choice? Begin contemplating what taking 100 percent responsibility might look like.

Every Upset Is an Opportunity to Learn

Upsets tick us off. It is hard to read "every upset is an opportunity to learn" and think *oh joy*. So ponder this a little more. Upsets trigger The Responsibility Process. If you have dedicated yourself to a responsibility practice, then you know the game is to catch yourself coping and get yourself to Responsibility. Doing so always results in learning and growth. Yes, you may become aware of something unpleasant that you wish wasn't true, and there will be discomfort and something to Confront. That is how we grow.

I don't want you to experience upsets. But I do want you to know that growth comes from overcoming challenges that cause you angst. To truly believe that every upset is an opportunity to learn means progressing from the fear of anxiety to embracing it because it signals an opportunity for breakthrough. So if you can reframe frustration and upset from a negative thing to simply an experience that triggers an opportunity for newfound freedom, choice, and power, you will be rewarded.

Responsibility Practice

Think of a current upset you are experiencing. What opportunity to learn is it providing?

Take It Easy on Yourself

High performers who are also newcomers to The Responsibility Process tend to get angry with themselves when they catch themselves in Lay Blame, Justify, Shame, or Obligation. Of course this is a conditioned response about *being* responsible, expecting better of yourself, holding yourself accountable to higher standards, etc. It's the cultural trance. When you do this, you land in Shame. Then to get out of Shame you make some rule about what you "have to" do to be better. By now you recognize that as Obligation. This pattern will not serve you.

So when you notice yourself in Lay Blame or any of the other coping states, remember to have compassion for self. We like to say, "Forgive yourself for being human." There is nothing wrong with you. Rather than chastise yourself for being wrong, congratulate yourself for catching it. Turn it into a win.

To operate from anger or chagrin is resisting the truth and will keep you stuck. Forgiveness of self is accepting the truth—that you are human and humans land in Lay Blame, Justify, Shame, etc. every time something goes wrong. Giving yourself a break in this way, repeatedly, every day allows you to learn and grow much more rapidly.

Responsibility Practice

See how many times a day you can catch yourself being angry or annoyed with yourself for blaming, justifying, shaming, etc., and then letting it go and forgiving yourself for coping with being human.

"What Do I Want?" Not "What Should I Do?"

Consider this. If you are like most people, you have learned to respond to many upsets with "What should I do?!" Check these examples:

"I just got called to our manager's office. That's never happened before. What should I do?"

"The electricity is off. What should I do?"

Get the picture? The phrase is a ubiquitous response to the anxiety of an upset, of something gone wrong. The fact that I'm even talking about it probably has you thinking, *Yeah, so what? It's normal.*"

Well, what if I told you that the question "What should I do?" is called up from a perspective of right and wrong, good and bad, or should and shouldn't? And that means it maps to the coping states of Shame and Obligation. Any search for the "right" answer does because you want to be right to be responsible.

Why do we automatically search for the right answer when we're anxious? Because we've been conditioned to. We've come of age during a time of unprecedented expansion of information, data, knowledge, and expertise. We've been taught that no matter what problem you have, someone has already solved it, and you just need to find that expert, tap into their wisdom, and follow it. You really don't have to think for yourself. You just have to be responsible enough to ask for the right answer and do as you are told.

Consider where that's gotten us. We've followed all of those shoulds and should-nots right into lives of being good and responsible with lots of unresolved problems. Prosperity on this planet has never been higher, yet anxiety, too, is at an all-time high. Note this headline: *Studies Show Normal Children Today Report More Anxiety than Child Psychiatric Patients in the 1950s.* "Normal" means to experience more and more anxiety. One of several reasons hypothesized for the high-stress levels in the article was pursuing the quick fix for problems. The quick fix helps us cope and alleviate some anxiety, but it never solves the real problem, and the anxiety returns again and again.[1]

Maybe it is time for a new question.

"What do I want?" is that better question. Or depending on the situation, "What do we want?" or even "Look at this mess. What do we want about this, right now, that we can do something about?"

"What do I want?" invites you to think for yourself. It invites you to own your role in the situation, and it invites you to see your path to a satisfying solution. Only asking that other question ("What should I do?") lets you avoid thinking for yourself or owning the situation.

"What do I want?" exercises your mind's Intention muscle, and by so doing, "What do I want?" maps to the mental state of Responsibility. If you are looking for a shortcut to Responsibility when things go wrong, ask yourself, "What do I want about this?"

Responsibility Practice

Catch yourself asking, "What should I do?" and change it to "What do I want about this situation?" Then forgive yourself and vow to catch yourself sooner next time.

Relearning How to Want

If The Responsibility Process is triggered when we have what we don't want, then freedom, power, and choice comes to us when we discover and pursue what we truly want. Unfortunately, most of us don't really know what that is. We speak of it vaguely like "success," "money," "a relationship," or "happiness." But your versions of these are not the same as mine. So the specifics matter.

Why don't we know what we really, really want? It's the cultural trance again. We grew up being told not to trust ourselves but to listen to well-intentioned parents, relatives, and teachers who told us what we *should* want. Be good. Fit in. Stay in school. Major in a field that's hiring. Go to work for a big stable company. And on, and on.

On the occasion of then California Governor Arnold Schwarzenegger receiving an honorary doctorate from the University of Southern California and giving the commencement address, Schwarzenegger ended his address with a griping five minutes on his six rules for success. Schwarzenegger grew up in Austria, took up bodybuilding, came to the USA, won seven titles as Mr. Olympia and five as Mr. Universe, has made more than fifty feature films having the lead role in most of them, and served as governor of California. Here he is talking about the first rule:

> *The first rule is: Trust yourself.*
>
> *And what I mean by that is, so many young people are get-ting so much advice from their parents and from their teachers and from everyone. But what is most important is that you have to dig deep down, dig deep down and ask yourselves, who do you want to be? Not what, but who.*
>
> *And I'm talking about not what your parents and teach-ers want you to be, but you. I'm talking about figuring out for yourselves what makes you happy, no matter how crazy it may sound to other people.*[2]

Everyone is born with unique predilections. That means you are dif-ferent from other people. You have your own genius, desires, joys, and passions. Denying them is living your life in Quit. Aligning to them brings fulfillment.

So, start exercising your *want* muscle. Yes, it is your power of Intention. The more you can align with who you truly are, the freer and more powerful you will be. How do you relearn how to want? I'll give you some ideas in the next four sections.

Responsibility Practice

On a scale of 1 to 10 with 1 being low and 10 being high, how much clarity do you have about what you want in your life, work, and relationships? If your answer falls toward the low range, join the crowd. These next sections are for you. If your answer falls toward the high range, congratulations. You are on your way.

How to Discover What You Really Want

Here is an exercise you can use to uncover what is most important in your life so that you can increasingly align yourself to it. It will take an hour or two for the first iteration. Then you can return to it from time to time to reexamine and realign.

Start by managing your energy and mood so you'll feel vibrant and alive while doing the exercise. For me, that would mean getting a good night's sleep, eating and hydrating well, and probably cycling twenty-five or thirty miles through the Texas Hill Country for inspiration and endorphins. Choose a supportive place where you can be undisturbed for a couple of hours. When I did this for the first time, I was on a cross-country flight in a window seat with no one next to me, looking out at the sun shining down on scattered clouds and the earth beneath them. It provided an expansive feeling. I imagined I was looking at my life from 35,000 feet.

The exercise involves generating lots of ideas, then working with those ideas. You can do this on a whiteboard, on paper, with sticky notes, or even in a text editor, word processor, outlining tool, or mind mapping app. Choose what feels supportive and creative to you.

Step I—Discovery. Begin by writing an exhaustive list of responses to this first question. Do not edit while you go. Do not judge your ideas as good or bad, right or wrong. This is an exercise in quantity, not quality. Just write response after response until you feel complete.

Here's the question: *What do you want to experience in your life in abundance on a daily basis?* (Copy this question into your organizer or reminder file so that you can find it when you are ready.)

In an hour I had written thirty-one statements and felt complete. By *complete* I mean I felt that everything that is most important to me was represented somewhere in those statements. I also noticed that I was repeating myself as I wrote more items, a sign that I had found most of my most important *wants*. Here's the good news, if I missed something, or if you miss something, the first time through, it will show up sooner or later and you can revise since this is a living exercise and always open to revision.

Here are a few of my statements:

- *Be a learner and a teacher*

- *Feel 100 percent free and at choice*

- *Enjoy the love of my family*

- *Score well at the business game*

- *Treat my mental and physical health as my most important assets*

Feel free to borrow any of mine that are true for you if they will help you get started. I have no doubt that you have plenty of your own.

Step 2—Organizing. Once you have an exhaustive list you may want to do a little editing or combining of a few of the phrases that are repeats. Your goal here is to keep your items focused on specific daily experiences (i.e., what you want to do, be, and have in abundance every day). Resist the urge to reduce them to one-word generalities like integrity, love, responsibility, etc.

147

Also resist the urge to dramatically reduce the quantity of statements. If a statement has an important element that would get lost if merged with another statement, then keep it separate.

In my case, when I cleaned up my list of thirty-one, I then had around twenty specific statements that represented what felt most important to me.

Step 3—Ordering. Now it is time to discover whether some of the statements are more important to you than others. This helps you focus, prioritize, and simplify your choices. Here is how to do it. Ask yourself this question: *If I could only experience one of these things in abundance on a daily basis, which would it be?*

That's correct. Only one.

I firmly believe you already know the answer at some level—if not consciously, then in your heart or spirit—so as you scan your list, just notice the statement that calls to you, that your eyes keep returning to, that you can feel in your heart or gut, or wherever you feel it. Resist logic, analysis, and what society, your parents, boss, or spouse would say. What matters is what your heart says.

Once you find that item, label it number one. Congratulate yourself for discovering it. Being aware of such a deep Intention is powerful alignment for your life.

Then repeat the prioritization question adding one to the number of things you could experience on a daily basis. If you are guided by a religious or spiritual path, you can add that in by asking *If God is so benevolent that I could experience two of these things in abundance on a daily basis, which one would be next?*

When you find that item, label it number two. Say yes silently to yourself to claim the win of aligning to a second deep Intention. Then, when you are ready, continue to look for a third, fourth, etc.

Once again, in this prioritization exercise, notice when you are feeling complete. In my case, after I had eleven statements, and was searching for a twelfth, I felt a little tired and burdened. None of the rest stood out as adding anything truly meaningful to the eleven I had already prioritized. Then I looked at my list of eleven and asked myself if it was complete. The answer was yes. At that moment, I realized that if I were experiencing those eleven things in abundance on a daily basis, then I would also be experiencing the remaining items because they appeared now to be a subset of the first eleven even though that was not apparent before I prioritized them. So I stopped at eleven.

Once you have prioritized the most important items into a list that feels complete, congratulate yourself again on the win, express your gratitude for the discovery, and enjoy the good feeling. Later you can decide what to do with this list.

Here's what I did with my list. First, as I faced this new prioritization of what I valued in life, I had the shocking realization that I was living my life every day as if number 11 on the list were number 1. Number 11 read *Score well at the business game.* Number 1 read *Treat my mental and physical health as my most important assets.* Fear and anxiety gripped me. I worried—But if I put anything else in front of earning a living, will I still be able to earn a living? And then I realized, number 11 is still on the list! It is still very important to me. If I put it in its proper place, then whatever happens must be what I truly want.

This is an example of Intention-Awareness-Confront leading to a new insight that reveals a powerful truth. I intended to discover what is truly important to me. I did discover it. And then I realized my daily thoughts and actions were out of alignment with it. It scared me to Confront what might happen if I realigned, and I faced that fear while looking for new insight, which I found.

Over the coming months and years, as I put my life priorities in order, I was able to make a living just fine, in fact, better than I had done before, because I wasn't compromising ten more important values to do it.

The second thing I did was to print out the list and post it where I would see it multiple times a day. This applies all Three Keys to Responsibility:

- **Intention**: I want to align my daily life and priorities to these eleven statements.

- **Awareness**: I grow increasingly aware of where I am aligning and where I am not, and

- **Confront**: I ask myself, "If I say this is important to me, why am I not aligning to it? Is it not true? Or am I afraid to trust it, thus resisting it? Or is something else going on?"

The third thing I did was to occasionally revise the list of eleven as I grew. After a few years, I realized that seven items on the list accounted for all the rest. Then a few years after that I reduced it further.

One final word about this exercise. You will notice that we asked, "What is important?" and we ended up with a list of core values. Why didn't we start by asking, "What are my values?" Simple. "Values" is a culturally loaded term. If we asked, "What are your values?" you would likely come up with what society says you should value.

Responsibility Practice

What is most important for you to experience in abundance on a daily basis? Since this exercise requires perhaps two hours the first time through, consider scheduling it on your calendar for some time in the coming week or two.

Craft Better Goals

Another way to relearn how to want is to examine your goals from a new perspective of Responsibility. The purpose of a true goal is to keep you in motion, pulling you toward the goal. As the goal pulls you to it, you take action, get feedback, learn and correct, or continue your course toward the goal. But many people's supposed goals don't put them in motion for some reason. That's because the so-called goals aren't really goals. They are "shoulds," but they don't actually pull you to them, so they aren't real goals. These are bad goals—bad because they don't work. If you want to acheive your goals, then start with what Bill McCarley, the father of The Responsibility Process research calls "Good Goals." According to McCarley, a good goal has the following characteristics:

1. ***Clarify Intention***. *The more clear you are about what you want and intend to accomplish, the better.*

2. ***Focus Attention***. *If you want to make sure something happens you must focus attention on it.*

3. ***Remove Obligation***. *Too many goals become a burden because people feel like they have to do them. Procrastination comes from Obligation.*

4. ***Generate Energy***. *Good goals lead to excitement, motivation, and a deep desire to do it!*[3]

Responsibility Practice

Assess your current goals in every area of your life against this Good Goal framework. Here are eight areas of your life to examine based on the *Co-Active Coaching* model, which I endorse and which many of my clients ascribe to (in case you are looking for a coach):

- Family & friends
- Significant other/Romance
- Fun & recreation
- Health
- Money
- Personal growth
- Physical environment
- Career[4]

If you have written goals, or a clear idea of what you have been striving toward, then be radically honest and rate each goal as a good goal or a bad goal using the four characteristics of Good Goals. Then Confront the bad goals to see what you can do to turn them into good goals or replace them.

If you do not have written goals, or are not clear about what your goals are, then ask yourself what you are striving to achieve in one of the eight areas of your life listed here. As you discover what it is, write it in the form of a good goal. Take your time with this exercise. If it takes you a week or a month or even a year to discover a good goal, it will be worth it.

Beyond Obligation

Listen to this story from Zach Nies the entrepreneur I mentioned in the last chapter. At the time, he was chief technology officer at a successful start-up Rally Software. Zach wrote, "Before studying The Responsibility Process and applying it to my life and work, I did not know there was a life beyond Obligation. I just thought work was a necessary burden. Almost two years later, I can confidently say it has had a tremendous positive impact on my leadership and teamwork skills. Two years ago I was struggling to find happiness leading a team of five people. Now, I am having fun leading a team of over sixty people. I am much more present and engaged at work and in life, and I enjoy higher levels of teamwork, trust, and collaboration with others."

Yes, there is a life beyond Obligation.

I've heard Zach's sentiments repeated hundreds of times by others who have developed a responsibility practice. Many patterns in life and work may look like a burden to you—something in which you are trapped and don't see a way out of —just something you must deal with to live. If so, there is nothing wrong with you. This perception of cause and effect in life is one of the persistent emotional diseases of so-called success. It is shared by billions of smart, educated, and well-intentioned people worldwide.

But I want to end that.

If your desire for a life beyond Obligation is strong enough, then simply believe that it is available to you. Doing the exercises in this chapter, and practicing responsibility daily, will gradually allow you to Confront what you currently may not be able to face, and that will lead to breakthroughs. Instead of giving in to Obligation, simply refuse to feel trapped, and that will lead your amazing mind to find new choices. Once again, the Catch Sooner Game will support you.

Responsibility Practice

Commit to getting beyond Obligation to Responsibility. Then every time you feel trapped or burdened, or think or say "have to (don't want to)," catch it with your Awareness. Remind yourself it is the coping state of Obligation. Acknowledge that you intend to get to Responsibility around this problem, that it could take a second, a minute, a month, or a year. Also acknowledge that you really don't "have to" at all. Instead you are freely choosing to keep your commitment even though you are not admitting it. Forgive yourself. Vow to catch yourself sooner next time. When you do this, your mind will begin looking for a new solution.

Clarify Your Needs, Wants, and Demands

Early on in most people's responsibility practice they encounter the confusion caused by three types of intentions. These are *needs*, *wants*, and *demands*. Getting clear on how you think about your intentions is a great source of personal power. Follow closely.

Intentions defined as needs lead us to feelings of lack or scarcity. If I say, "I need a new suit," then my mind pictures that I am lacking something. Needs are motivating but in an anxiety-producing way.

Let's take an extreme example. When I was studying for a scuba certification as a teen, one of the exercises was to learn to clear my snorkel while someone on the side of the pool was pouring water into the top of it. Yes, regular access to oxygen is important to living. However by practicing this snorkel-clearing exercise, we were learning to remain calm and not panic when we experienced a temporary absence of access to oxygen. I was also a lifeguard, and I learned that the human body is nearly the same consistency as the water we swim in. Therefore it takes just a little strength and skill to remain afloat. And that means that drowning while swimming is often the result of a person panicking when he gets a gulp of water in the airway.

So, we see that an extreme need induces panic. It is easy to see that a less extreme need is still defined as a lack, a scarcity. The more we define our intentions as needs, the more unnecessary angst we create for ourselves.

Intentions defined as "wants" lead us to feelings of joy, anticipation, and abundance. If I say "I want a new suit," my mind envisions choices, possibilities, and paths to obtainment.

Try it. In your internal voice (that's the voice in your head that just said, *What internal voice? I don't have an internal voice.*) make each of the following statements, one at a time, and then listen for your internal feelings and responses:

- I need to finish this report. / I want to finish this report.

- I need to go to the store. / I want to go to the store.

- I need a red Porsche. / I want a red Porsche.

- I need to find love. / I want to find love.

Some people who try this do not discern a significant difference at first. In fact, some people think it is silly. However many others feel the difference right away, and the difference is remarkable.

So what is the takeaway? If you want to feel better, more joyous, more in charge, more free, then turn all your needs into wants.

Think about it. Society teaches us to be needy. We unconsciously say "I need" when we could say "I want." And a goal of consumer marketing is to introduce us to new needs we didn't even know we had, which make us feel like we lack even more!

Try this mind trick. Tell yourself that science and religion each tell you that all our needs are met. Abraham Maslow says so with his hierarchy of needs. And the Bible, Koran, and other great texts promise that God provides. That means I have no needs, only wants. This reframe works. Now it is a Catch Sooner Game to catch yourself saying, "I need to lose weight and get in shape." Recognize this statement as an anxiety-producing bad goal, and reframe it to "I want to be a fit, toned, 130 pounds."

Now that you understand needs versus wants, there is one more type of Intention to understand: demand. A demand is something that will depress you if it is not pursued and met. As an example, think of the spoiled sixteen-year-old who throws a fit until you break down and buy her the $200 designer jeans she demanded because her life would be ruined if she had to show up at the party in anything already in her closet.

You wouldn't succumb to such a demand from a teen? Good for you. If it is truly a demand of hers, then she'll likely find a way to earn the money for the jeans.

Be careful of the demands you place on yourself and others, especially if the demands are superficial. If you demand to belong to the best club in town, drive the fanciest car, have all the best wardrobe, etc., but the economics of your life don't support that, then you will make yourself miserable.

I've learned to be selective in my life demands. I have just a few. For one, I demand to experience freedom, power, and choice daily. The thought of not having that depresses me. For another, I demand to earn a living and support my family by doing what I love, which is studying and teaching how personal responsibility works in the mind. There was a point where I *needed* to earn a living, and I *wanted* to study and teach Responsibly, but I was afraid I would not be accepted and would fail. That incongruent need and want drove me crazy for a while. Eventually I simply demanded of myself that I find a way to make a living by following my highest value and calling—to master and teach The Responsibility Process.

I won't kid you and say that from that moment it was a snap to earn the living I wanted to provide for my family. There have been plenty of ups and downs. However, it has worked out, and I can't imagine a better and more fulfilling life.

Responsibility Practice

Set an Intention to better understand your needs, wants, and demands; to turn your needs into wants; and to be selective about your demands. Knowing what's most important to you, from the exercise you just completed in this chapter, will support you here.

For another application, catch yourself using the word *need* and change it to *want*.

Focus On the Essential

In his best-selling book *The 80/20 Principle: The Secret to Achieving More with Less*, successful management consultant and entrepreneur Richard Koch claims that the one true principle of highly effective people and organizations is that 80 percent of results flow from just 20 percent of the causes.[5] This is widely understood as the Pareto principle named after the Italian economist Vilfredo Pareto who observed that 20 percent of the peapods in his garden contained 80 percent of the peas, and that 80 percent of the land in Italy was owned by 20 percent of the population.[6]

Applied to business, it is often found that 80 percent of a company's revenues come from just 20 percent of the products, or that 20 percent of the sales force produces 80 percent of the sales. Applied to life happiness and success, it implies that we can achieve more by focusing on less. How can you do that?

Focus on the essential, says Greg McKeown, author of *Essentialism: The Disciplined Pursuit of Less*. If you feel stretched too thin, or overworked and underutilized, you are likely producing only 20 percent of desired results from 80 percent of your time, energy, and efforts. What does McKeown suggest? Decide what results you truly want to generate, then decide what is absolutely essential to produce those results, and eliminate all the nonessential.[7]

In his book *Anything You Want*, Derek Sivers, the entrepreneur mentioned in the introduction offers a fabulous exercise for identifying the essential and nonessential in life, and it calls on The Responsibility Process. Here are the steps (in my words):

Step 1. Identify all your commitments. Make a list of every commitment, promise, initiative, project, goal, and objective in every area of your life. It can be a commitment to yourself or to another. Just write it down.

Step 2. Sort your commitments into three columns. The three columns are *No*, *Yes*, and *Hell Yes*. Since each is something you are already doing, you won't have anything in the No column at first. When applying The Responsibility Process, Hell Yes items represent true wants and demands, good goals, and commitments you really own. Yes items are probably shoulds, have to's, bad goals, etc. If this step generates new Awareness and Confront, then the exercise is working as it should.

Step 3. Empty the Yes column. That's right. Sivers says eliminate half-hearted commitments. He says make everything in your life either a No or a Hell Yes.[8]

Like every professional, I sometimes overcommit. Sometimes it is all Hell Yes things. That's actually a good problem to have. The way I solve it is to confess to those who depend on me that I'm oversubscribed and want their help reprioritizing.

How do I determine if something is a Hell Yes or just a Yes? For me, it's pretty easy. I feel a sense of ownership and responsibility for the Hell Yeses. I am pulled toward them. The Yes items feel like Obligation.

What do I do with Yeses? If I can't get past Obligation with an item to Responsibility, then I look to turn it into a No. Maybe it doesn't need doing, or maybe it's someone else's Hell Yes.

When you know that you are free, powerful, and at choice, there's always a way. We control what we let into our lives, so saying yes and no becomes important. As professionals, we're likely very good at saying yes to the tasks and assignments we're given. The trick is to not feel trapped by those and to examine what you're saying yes to as well as the higher purpose behind that yes.

The Hell Yeses are for what really defines you. How much more satisfying could your life be if you said: "Hell yes! I want to do that" versus "Yes, I guess I could get that done"?

I like to cycle. I'm a roadie. That means I put in lots of miles on a light-weight road bike. My mapmyride app says I've logged 9,946 miles (and burned 628,000 calories) since I started using the app. Riding is a *Hell Yes*. And I live in riding paradise, in rural, south central Texas in a small town called Comfort. I can leave my home office, be on my bike in five minutes, and ride for two or three hours on roads with very little car traffic. I do it routinely, and I do it alone most of the time. It is a highly integrated (i.e., leveraged) use of my time because not only am I getting amazing exercise doing something I love in a beautiful place, I am also either listening to audiobooks or simply letting my mind wander across my relationships, goals, projects, challenges, and problems. I make a lot of progress in life and work in a couple of hours on my bike.

People frequently ask me if I am doing an upcoming organized ride, one of those big events attracting hundreds of riders often raising money for a cause. For the past dozen years, I've been a clear No on organized rides. I'm even a No about getting together with others and riding if it requires any organizing, driving to meet up, or waiting around for people to gather. Why? Because the ratio of invested time and attention to benefit isn't there for me. Riding is essential. Riding with others is not.

Responsibility Practice

Step 1. Identify all your commitments.

Step 2. Sort your commitments into three columns: No, Yes, and Hell Yes.

Step 3. Work over time to empty the Yes column by figuring out how to make each entry a Hell Yes or a No.

Cleaning Up Our Messes

Do you ever make mistakes? Of course you do. You are human, and humans set out with good plans and intentions and then life happens. We make a decision that doesn't turn out, or we make an agreement with another person and then blow it. It happens all the time. In the previous section, I mentioned becoming overcommitted and how I handle it. Dealing with it by owning up and cleaning up our messes is critical.

Operating from Responsibility when things go wrong means owning the consequences of our actions and cleaning up after ourselves. Why? Well, for one thing, we learn from it. And for another, we maintain our integrity and the trust and confidence of others who are affected by our mistakes. Responsibility is about the cause-and-effect forces in our life. It is about how we integrate with the world in which we live. When people and businesses around us mess up and cause unwanted effects for others, we expect them to own up to it, take responsibility, and make it "right" by cleaning up the problem and making restitution.

People who practice responsibility would have it no other way when they make a mistake. They want to own it and clean it up. Here's how:

Step 1. Acknowledge. Let's say you and I had an appointment to meet for lunch today and you forgot. Now you could try to deny it to yourself saying, "Well, we didn't actually specify," or you could cope by thinking to yourself *Maybe Christopher forgot too, so I won't look foolish.* However we know that acceptance is the fastest path to Responsibility, so the thing to do is acknowledge that you blew it. And the person you need to acknowledge it to is yourself. If we can acknowledge our mistakes to ourselves then we can acknowledge them to others.

Step 2. Apologize. As soon as possible after the mistake, apologize. And do it boldly. Don't be wimpy and squirmy about it. Say, "I apologize to you. You did not deserve that from me." I don't need to tell you that humans can be really poor at apologizing. We say, "*If* you were offended, then I'm sorry." How passive! That's a conditional apology. It is not owning what you did. The value of a clear and bold apology is that the affected party will more likely understand that you completely own what happened and will learn from it. That makes you worth continuing to trust and have confidence in.

Step 3. Ask. Sincerely ask, "What can I do to make amends." This demonstrates that the relationship is important to you and that you are willing to invest in returning relationship trust and confidence to the premistake level. Again, don't come from Shame and with a tome of self-pity saying, "Is there anything I can do?" Come from Responsibility and say, "What can I do to make this right with you?" Then listen and either do it or negotiate a win/win. If the other party says, "Don't worry about it; it's no big deal" instead of releasing a sigh of relief, say, "Are you sure? Because I don't want there to be any residue of resentment. I blew it, and I want to clean it up so we can move forward."

Step 4. Recommit. Finally, apply the Catch Sooner Game by recommitting yourself to the relationship. Let the other party know that you are making a change in the way you treat your agreements with them so you will be more reliable in the future.

You can take this four-step cleanup framework with you everywhere in your life. If you engage in it sincerely, it works wonders. As an exercise, ask yourself if there are some mistakes, broken agreements, or messes that you have not yet completely owned and cleaned up, and then take steps to do so.

Responsibility Practice

Identify where you have failed to keep an agreement or some other mistake or mess you created that had an impact on another person. Clean it up.

Claiming Wins Builds the Power of Intention

Often when people get what they want, they celebrate spontaneously with fist bumps or high fives. Think about it. You give a successful presentation at a meeting, and on your way off stage back to your seat you do a silent fist pump, saying to yourself yes. Or maybe you pull off a prank on a colleague and claim the win for yourself when it goes as planned. You see this all the time in sports, when players celebrate a good play or a good try. You see it with kids when they meet an Intention, and they say, "Oh yeah, way to go."

Claiming wins is a foundational practice for Responsibility. I've saved it for last in this chapter to make it the capstone. It is that important.

We define a win as an Intention met. It is something you intended to happen and it did, or it is something you intended to not happen and it didn't. In each case, it is a win.

Most of us drastically downplay our everyday wins and successes—to our own detriment. We focus on losses all day long, which sends us into victimhood. We gripe, we complain, commiserate, and think, *Why me?* We *hate* the alarm clock. We *have* to go to the *stupid* meeting. We'll have less time for lunch because we *need* to run errands. Loss, loss, loss, loss, loss.

The truth is that we are in charge of our choices—even if we don't admit it—but instead of seeing all the ways in which we are free, have power, and are operating from the position of choice all day long, we pay attention to all the ways that we are imprisoned, powerless, and without choice.

Let's turn that around. Let's start claiming wins. Each of the sections in this chapter offered you an exercise or practice. That means there is an opportunity to act on an Intention. If you want to accelerate your progress, start claiming wins. Do it frequently. Do it as they occur. It doesn't require fanfare—and certainly does not require bragging or boasting to others about how great you are. It just requires an acknowledgment to yourself that you intended for something to happen and it did.

As I write this, I am using a focusing technique called pomodoro. It has been used for years by creatives like copywriters and software programmers to maintain focus on a task. To use it, you set a timer for twenty-five minutes during which you work diligently on your project. When twenty-five minutes is up, you can take a five-minute break to do something else, or you can set the timer for twenty-five minutes and go again. For every pomodoro I complete, I claim a small win. Sometimes I can complete ten pomodoros in a five hour stretch. That's a win. I wrote 2,000 words today. That's a win. And I got a bike ride in. That's a win. I enjoyed family dinner with my wife and boys. That's a win. And I broke through a stuck point on a problem. That's a win.

Now you. Think of a win. It doesn't need to be large. A win is not a size; it is an Intention met. Did you intend to read this sentence? Congratulations.

The more you practice responsibility, the more you will be living intentionally, which means you will notice your wins. And the more you realize how much you are winning, the greater your desire will be to own your life. Here are a few tips about claiming wins.

The cultural trance has us focused on losing rather than winning. When we start claiming wins, we think it is petty or ridiculous, or even boasting or bragging. So we edit our wins.

Recently, while claiming wins with a team, a colleague said, "I can't think of any." Since I practice winning every minute of every day, this statement revealed how much this person focused on losing rather than winning. He clearly saw himself "at effect" with no choice in life rather than "at cause." So I asked again with more permission to look for a win. I said, "If you could possibly think of any win of any size, what might it be?"

I saw him pause and think. I could tell he was mulling over ideas of potential wins in his mind, and then he would shake it off signaling, "This isn't impressive enough to share." In other words, he was self-editing. He was denying himself wins! That filter comes from a society that teaches us delayed gratification and that we only deserve to claim the biggest of wins. We tell ourselves two limiting beliefs:

- Small wins really aren't wins.

- The only wins that matter are huge wins.

Neither of those statements is true! Self-editing sabotages our ability to act with Responsibility. Remember, a "win" is anything you intended to happen that did indeed happen and anything you intended to not happen that did not happen.

Here are some examples of met intentions I've heard recently from my clients:

- "I finished the proposal. That's a win."

- "I have a win. I intended to walk two miles during my lunch break every day this week, and I did."

- "I intended to not crash the build yesterday, and I didn't. That's a win."

- "My win is that I intended to pitch management on a continuous improvement experiment, and I did."

It is good practice to notice your requirements for acknowledging something as a win. Did you consider—but discard—many intentions you'd met because they seemed so small? Consider this: I intended to wake up this morning, and I did. That's a win.

Did you permit yourself to see only one or two wins because you thought you didn't deserve more? If so, I invite you to deserve more. When we edit what wins we allow ourselves to celebrate, we will be more likely to stay stuck coping with crap instead of experiencing freedom, power, and choice. This goes beyond positive reinforcement; it is recognizing how frequently we really do have exactly what we want—and that's a win—so we learn to do it again and again and recognize when it happens.

Responsibility Practice

At least once a day, claim at least five (or ten, or twenty) wins from the past twenty-four hours. I do this in the morning, after waking up but before getting out of bed. I review yesterday looking for the first five wins I can recall. I think to myself *I intended to make significant progress on the book writing, and I did. That's a win. I intended to ride, and I did. That's a win.* Claiming at least five wins puts me in a mental state of gratitude and Responsibility, a powerful way to start the day. Some of my clients prefer to do it after they go to bed and before drifting off to sleep. When you do it is less important than that you do it.

Summary

This chapter was devoted to leading yourself first by applying Responsibility to your experience of everyday life. We applied The Responsibility Process, the Three Keys of Responsibility, and the Catch Sooner Game to lots of everyday life situations. We learned:

- The Responsibility Process works only when it is self-applied,

- To wake up and expose the cultural trance,

- Every upset is an opportunity to learn,

- To take it easy on ourselves

- To ask "What do I want?" instead of "What should I do?"

- We relearned how to want, and we learned how to:

- Discover what we really want

- Craft good goals

- Reach beyond Obligation

- Clarify our needs, wants, and demands

- Focus on the essential

- Clean up our messes, and

- Claim wins to build the power of Intention

In the next chapter, we raise the bar for relating with others as we explore how to lead from Responsibility so others will step up to Responsibility. And if you feel full with the practices from this chapter, and not yet ready to raise the bar, I applaud you. Focus on the most important practices from this chapter until you feel some mental energy to proceed to the next chapter.

7

Sharing Responsibility, Sharing Leadership

Do you share responsibility with others for things that are larger than each of you and also depend on the care, investment, and responsiveness of all? Of course you do. Maybe it is a project, a start-up business, a cross-functional initiative, a family, an informal weekly sporting match, or a community group like a church or a theater. We use a variety of names for such relationships. We call them collaborations, teamwork, projects, partnering, community, marriage, and family—all examples of sharing responsibility with others for something important to each of you.

This chapter examines shared-responsibility situations through the lenses of The Responsibility Process, the Three Keys to Responsibility, and Catch Sooner so that you can navigate them with greater clarity and confidence. When such situations go well, it is a joy to be a part of them. Valuable outcomes are achieved. Strong bonds and memories are made.

Trust is extended. Responsibility is easily taken, and leadership is shared naturally. Most of us who have experienced this want to experience more of it.

When such situations don't go well, it is terribly frustrating. Results are not achieved. Relationships decay and break. Trust is withdrawn. Responsibility is avoided. Leadership and direction is fought over, or neglected.

This is the fuzzy, complex, maddeningly frustrating, and immensely gratifying world of shared responsibility. I've been fascinated with the dynamics of shared responsibility since 1988 while working on my dissertation—a study of competing loyalties between scientists, engineers, marketers, and managers in the first US R&D consortium. My 2001 book *Teamwork Is an Individual Skill: Getting Your Work Done when Sharing Responsibility* detailed what I learned in those thirteen years. I took the position that "a team is a group of individuals responding successfully to the opportunity presented by shared responsibility." I also took the view that you can behave in ways that encourage others to step up with you to shared responsibility. Fourteen years later my view has not changed. Being effective in shared-responsibility situations calls on your Intention to build and align relationships around a specific larger purpose. It demands your Awareness of how groups naturally step up to the opportunity presented by shared responsibility and how they don't. And it calls for you to Confront your own Responsibility for the success or failure of the larger whole.

I will not rehash the contents of *Teamwork Is an Individual Skill* in this chapter. Instead, I will highlight the most important dynamics and perspectives affecting success or failure in shared-responsibility situations so that you can be aware and make your choices.

Responsibility Practice

Think of a range of shared-responsibility situations in your life, work, and relationships. Think of at least one that is going, or did go, extremely well. And think of at least one that is going, or did go, poorly. Then fill in a couple more somewhere between those two. As you explore this chapter, assess these situations based on what you are learning.

The Main Dynamics: Alignment and Integration

Alignment and integration are the most important dynamics to attend to in shared-responsibility situations. *Alignment* refers to the directional focus of people's efforts. If people in a shared-responsibility situation are not aligned, there will be frustration, suspicion, and conflict. Unless people recognize this and know how to positively address it, the likelihood is high that parties will step away from Responsibility rather than take it.

Think of the four tires on a car. When aligned, the car rolls smoothly. When not aligned, there is tension, loss of momentum, and unnecessary wear and tear. The way to achieve alignment in shared-responsibility situations is with a shared goal or purpose, the more inspiring the better. The challenge is to ensure that it is truly shared by all and not just by one or a few. If the purpose is not truly shared, there isn't alignment.

The other main dynamic at work in shared-responsibility situations is *integration*—the degree to which members operate with shared values, principles, and beliefs that support and protect the whole as well as the parts. Some would call this trust, transparency, integrity, or even relationship. It is all of those. It is also participation and inclusion, honoring differences, fairness, community, caring equally for all members, protecting other people's boundaries (or vulnerabilities), and never being the first to defect on the group or on another member of the group.

To provide leadership in shared-responsibility situations, you will focus on achieving and maintaining alignment and integration. In the sections that follow, I will delve a little deeper into these dynamics.

Responsibility Practice

In the range of shared-responsibility situations that you identified earlier, consider how alignment and integration, or the lack of alignment and integration, played a role in the success or failure of each situation. Also consider how effective leadership—likely collaborative in nature—contributed to people aligning and integrating in the success cases. What about the leadership—or lack of it—in the unsuccessful cases?

You Are a Trim Tab

I once had the privilege to interview all the members of a large engineering program that had failed. The employer was well known for hiring only the top 10 percent of engineering graduates from only the top engineering colleges, so the failure was of course embarrassing. I asked everyone I interviewed, "To what do you attribute your participation in this failed program?" The number-one response was "I guess I got put on a bad team."

I heard this helpless Justify from smart and well-intentioned professionals wherever I traveled to study and teach team leadership skills. It struck me that part of our cultural trance is that individuals do not feel responsible for the quality of their experience at work. They feel "at effect" rather than "at cause."

So many people assume they can't make much of a difference in groups unless they are given authority over others in the group. However in group settings, these same individuals admit seeing either a positive or negative difference that others make. So what's up? It's a fairly straightforward matter of perception that I call the "can't see myself" effect. We can perceive how a group that we are in might be different with or without each other member. However we either can't or don't perceive how that group would be different without us. We see the impact everyone else is having but don't recognize our own.

When these people become aware that they must alter the dynamic of every group they are in just by being there (because others do), they become more Intentional about their participation. They want to be a positive force.

A useful metaphor here is the trim tab. A trim tab is a small lever on the outer edge of a larger lever such as a ship's rudder (figure 7.1). It could take great force to turn the rudder against the onrushing water. Yet, with much less force, the pilot can engage the tiny trim tab on the edge of the

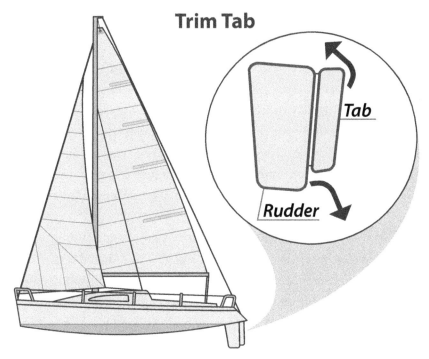

Figure 7.1. *Trim Tab.*

rudder to do the work of turning the huge rudder into the flow, and the rudder turns the huge ship. So, through the use of leverage, the tiny force of a trim tab naturally results in turning the huge ship.

In every shared-responsibility situation, you are a trim tab whether you know it or not. There are many small things you can do that move the dynamics toward a positive shared-responsibility situation. In the next section, we'll look at the most important place to start.

Responsibility Practice

Can you identify where you or others have been trim tabs in shared-responsibility situations—where fairly small behaviors have resulted in large dynamics or impacts to the shared-responsibility situation?

Take 100 Percent Responsibility for Every Relationship

Remember those people who "got put on a bad team"? What you and I know is that they chose, created, or attracted that situation. They just weren't owning it. If they owned it—if they took 100 percent responsibility for the quality and productivity of every relationship at work—they might show up differently. They would be aware of alignment and integration. They would hold an Intention to create supportive conditions. They would Confront the complex reality of shared-responsibility situations and engage their trim tab thinking early.

So the precondition for finding yourself in more and more situations where people step up to the opportunity presented by a shared responsibility is to take 100 percent responsibility for the quality and productivity of every relationship in life and work. When you begin thinking about taking 100 percent responsibility for the quality and productivity of every relationship, something else happens. You also begin demanding to be in great relationships, on great teams, and in great communities. And when you do that, you challenge yourself to be worthy of a great team or a great family. And when you show up as someone who both demands and is worthy of a positive experience in shared-responsibility situations, then you show up as an effective and positive trim tab.

Responsibility Practice

Consider committing to a Catch Sooner cycle for taking 100 percent responsibility for the quality and productivity of every relationship. Intend to have fabulously aligned and integrated relationships. Develop your Awareness of relationship dynamics that move toward or away from alignment and integration. Confront what you, as a trim tab, could do to improve the quality and productivity of every relationship.

Responsibility Is Leadership

There is good reason why people who practice responsibility become better leaders. Noel Tichy in *The Leadership Engine: How Winning Companies Build Leaders at Every Level* describes leadership as taking ownership for a situation, opportunity, or problem, and then mobilizing resources for action.[1] And he is not the only one. Many leadership researchers have equated leadership with Responsibility. Leadership starts with a feeling of Responsibility for something larger than you, thus it calls on you to attract others to the opportunity, situation, or problem to effectively address it.

This means leadership is innate in each of us. Since we are born with The Responsibility Process on board, we all have the capacity to lead ourselves and others when we operate from Responsibility. To the extent that we practice and master Responsibility in our lives, we are drawn more and more toward the experiences and results we intend. Growing as leaders is a natural by-product.

The tired old debate about whether leaders are born or made is put to rest. Leaders make themselves by routinely taking Responsibility for and stepping up to larger and larger challenges.

Responsibility Practice

How have you shown leadership naturally because you cared about a problem, situation, or opportunity that was larger than you? As you stepped up to Responsibility, you likely inspired others to join you.

Shared Responsibility Is Shared Leadership

When people in a shared-responsibility situation step up to high levels of ownership, you also see high levels of shared leadership. People take turns leading and following each other in different aspects of the initiative. In this case, leadership is not about title, assignment, control, or ego. Instead it is about service and contribution. A team or family member sees a shared problem or opportunity that she can do something about, so she takes initiative—responsibility—and demonstrates leadership. And because she is solving a shared problem or advancing a shared opportunity, the others swarm in to support—follow—her. This is the natural flow of high-performance dynamics: serve and be served, support and be supported, lead and be led.

An emerging area of leadership research calls this "distributed leadership." Distributive leadership is unique in that it does not describe qualities or characteristics of the individual. Instead it describes a quality of the system (i.e., the context or the culture) where leadership is distributed among the members of the system.[2] This supports the notion that leadership is a by-product of stepping up to Responsibility. It also supports the notion that leadership is innate in all of us.

Responsibility Practice

Think of a time when you saw a hundred small acts of leadership, shared widely among members of a group, emerge and flow naturally to produce results that mattered. How did it feel? What were the dynamics? What conditions do you think fell into place that allowed that to happen? Finally, are those conditions something you might put in place intentionally?

Your Greatest Source of Power

Most people are unaware of their greatest source of power. The brilliant economist Kenneth Boulding, one of the fathers of general systems theory, studied how you and I accrue and use power in an economic system. As you continue to build your thinking as a trim tab, you may be surprised to learn that there are only three sources of power:

- **Authority power:** Boulding called this "power over" and also classified it as "threat" power;

- **Exchange power:** Boulding called this "power to" or "power by," which you and I know as bargaining power;

- **Integrative power:** Boulding called this "power with" and described it as your ability to attract others to you using only your ideas and actions to accomplish something greater than you could do alone.

Your total power is determined by how you combine and use, or misuse, these three sources.[3]

Of the three sources of power, Boulding said that two of them are celebrated and sought after in our society, and one of them goes virtually unrecognized. Can you guess which two are celebrated and sought after?

The first two: authority and exchange power. We are taught to strive for positional authority and to go for the money. Integrative power remains relatively ignored and invisible. (If we are unaware of it, we may be denying our greatest source of power.)

Also, Boulding said two of the power sources are limited because their value depends on scarcity, and one of the sources is available in unlimited abundance. And it is the same two, authority and exchange power, which are limited. Only your integrative power is unlimited; although, you may choose to limit it, and you're the only one who can.

Of these three sources of power in an economic system, your greatest source of power may go unrecognized, underdeveloped, and underused. Let's take responsibility for changing that. Understand that you need no authority power or exchange power to demonstrate leadership. In fact, those sources of power can be hindrances because they are easily applied in manipulative ways that incentivize coping rather than growing.

Some people talk about leading from a position of "no power." They mean leading from a position of no threat power. You always have plenty of power even when you think you don't. You have far more power and ability than you usually give yourself credit for.

Responsibility Practice

Think of a time when you accomplished plenty with little or no authority and little or no budget to exchange, yet you attracted others and produced results together. How was this an example of your integrative power?

Set Up Positive Interdependence

The single greatest lever for transforming any group into a team is the feeling that "we are in the same boat together." This is both an alignment and integration issue.

Why?

When people feel like they are in the same boat together, their behavior toward one another is naturally more open, supportive, and collaborative. They are more willing than otherwise to give and ask for help, to extend trust, and to lead and follow each other.

Imagine Sally and Jane out in the middle of a large lake. Jane notices a significant leak in the canoe next to Sally's left foot. Does Jane:

1. Pull out her cell phone, dial her other best friend, and with a snicker say, "Sally's got a leak in her boat"?

2. Ignore it?

3. Say, "Hey Sally, we've got a problem"?

I don't think you need me to answer this for you.

But now, let's say John and Stan are out in the lake each in their own boats. John notices a leak in Stan's boat. Are you as sure about what John would do as you are about what Jane would do?

I bet you aren't.

The dynamic at work in these vignettes is called "outcome interdependence."

Consider Jane and Sally in the canoe. Where effort and reward is concerned, they are positively interdependent. That means that when Jane works hard, Sally benefits, and when Sally works hard, Jane benefits. And, if Jane slacks off, Sally loses, so Sally might get on Jane's case right away. Thus real-time feedback—both acknowledgment and correction—occur when people feel like they are in the same boat together. It is either win together or lose together; there is no other outcome.

Now consider John and Stan. Without more information about the context of their being in separate boats on the lake, we really can't say.

But let's say they are each there alone. John has little investment in what Stan does, and vice versa. They are independent.

But what if John and Stan are competitive members of the rowing club. They are each vying for the club championship of the decade, and there are big stakes and bragging rights. John and Stan are negatively interdependent. That is, the closer John gets to his goal, the harder it is for Stan to obtain his goal. And vice versa of course. Consider also that the more John slacks off or experiences misfortune, the easier that makes Stan's goal of winning—and that might make Stan feel good, even if they are in the same club!

What's important is the perception of positive, negative, or neutral (independent) interdependence in the relationships. When shared-responsibility situations go well, you will always see positive interdependence in place, and when shared-responsibility situations go badly, this is usually missing.

To take a stand for positive interdependence, ask the others who share responsibility with you, "What is our shared outcome (or purpose or goal)?" Here is a more specific question you can ask:

- "What must we do together that:

- is larger than any of us,

- requires all of us, and

- none of us can claim as an individual victory until it is done?"

Keep the question in front of the group until you are all looking at each other, nodding your heads in agreement, and smiling about the singular answer you share and understand. Then take the win. It is a tremendous source of leverage.

Responsibility Practice

Think of shared-responsibility situations you have been in. In which ones was there a clear shared outcome that caused perceptions of positive interdependence? In which situations was this lacking? In each case, how did that affect (impact) the dynamics of interdependence and outcomes?

Play a Bigger Game

At the height of the Cold War in 1968, Dr. R. Buckminster Fuller authored *Operating Manual for Spaceship Earth* in which he described what would happen if the people on the bow of a ship at sea and the people at the stern of the ship did not like each other and started lobbing bombs from bow to stern and stern to bow.[4] Of course the ship sinks. His point is that when, in a shared-responsibility situation, we pick a win-lose fight, the outcome is really lose-lose even if we "win."

Just two years earlier, in 1966, our *Three Faces of Power* author Kenneth Boulding had published a research paper called "The Economics of the Coming Spaceship Earth." Boulding compared our planet's "cowboy economy" of resource extraction and environmental pollution with a proposed "spaceman economy" where we collectively view Earth as a ship traveling through space requiring a cyclical economic system re-using everything.[5]

Fuller and Boulding were building on the political economist Henry George's ship analogy, who in 1879 wrote: "It is a well-provisioned ship, this on which we sail through space. If the bread and beef above decks seem to grow scarce, we but open a hatch and there is a new supply, of which before we never dreamed. And very great command over the services of others comes to those who as the hatches are opened are permitted to say, 'This is mine!'"[6]

Environmentalism and social responsibility have deep roots. We can also see that extracting something—whether from the planet or from another—produces a net zero gain to the larger system. This is win-lose thinking, also known as scarcity thinking. We assume that value is fixed and that we must compete for "our fair share." For us to win, we must extract something from another. For us to get more, someone has to get less. "That's just the way it is," we say.

Or is it?

The concept of scarcity is counterbalanced by the concept of enough, also known as abundance. This is the point of view that value isn't necessarily a fixed pie and that, in fact, value can be generated. Through the process of innovation, we resolve a temporary scarcity of supply—of not having enough—by finding alternative ways to provide the same or better value for less energy, materials, or effort.

Using the lenses of scarcity and enough, let's take a look at how well we are doing. Instead of comparing ourselves to the person on the next machine at the gym, let's look at how well we are doing compared to the wealthiest monarchs on the planet just fifteen decades ago. By 2020, 3.2 billion people on the planet will be living by middle-class standards.[7] That means 3.2 billion people will be enjoying a standard of living far greater than the wealthiest few kings, queens, and other aristocrats enjoyed just 150 years ago—an astonishing expansion of quality of life. What do so many of us have today that no one had 150 years ago? Let's start with indoor plumbing and air conditioning. Do you appreciate these or take them for granted? How about transportation, communications, connectivity, and grocery stores with miles of shelves stocked with everything imaginable?

How about health care? The average life expectancy in 1865 was about forty years. Today it is seventy-eight years, plus two years for women, minus two for men. That means if you are forty years or older, you are living free years by virtue of when you were born. Here's a question to Confront: What are you doing with your life? Are you playing scarcity games acting as if you don't have enough? Or do you realize that you actually have an abundant, joyous existence with which to do something meaningful?

A terrific example of scarcity thinking versus abundance thinking is the conscious capitalism practiced by Whole Foods founder and co-CEO John Mackey as an alternative to what he calls crony capitalism. In *crony capitalism*, the business exists to maximize shareholder value. When conflicts arise between the interests of the investors and the interests of any other group, tradeoffs are generally made in the interest of the investor. A by-product of this is that other constituents like employees, suppliers, and customers learn that they had better grab what little they can too!

In *conscious capitalism* the business exists to support the interests of the entire ecosystem. Whole Foods defines six players in its ecosystem:

- Customers

- Employees

- Suppliers

- Investors

- Communities

- Governments

Their Win6 philosophy states that they will pursue win/win/win/win/win/win with these six players in their purpose, strategy, goals, policies, and practices. Mackey and coauthor Raj Sisodia write: "A key difference between a traditional business and a conscious business is that in the former, managers routinely make trade-offs among stakeholders. A good manager is seen as one who makes trade-offs that are more advantageous to the investor stakeholders than to others. Conscious businesses understand that if we look for trade-offs, we *always* will find them. *If we look for synergies across stakeholders, we can usually find those too.*"[8] The evidence presented in *Conscious Capitalism* shows that businesses operating with such a "bigger game" approach outperform traditional business by a wide margin. That means the investors' wins are even bigger.

An entrepreneur friend was describing his new venture to me. As he described it, I found myself leaning farther back in my chair staring up into space trying to grasp the enormity of the vision. I asked him, how do you intend to accomplish all of this? His answer illustrated the idea of choosing a bigger game. "Oh, I don't," he said, "I'm just going to grab a piece of it and enjoy the ride." What I learned from this is that if you want to attract lots of great partners, then use your integrative power to develop the largest vision you can think of. People who align with your vision will show up to support you. Enjoy the ride.

Responsibility Practice

To recondition your sense of "normal" from an overly developed sense of scarcity to a healthy sense of enough, consider applying your Intention, Awareness, and Confront to designing, leading, and participating only in win/win games of life, relationship, and business. When offered fabulous opportunities, examine the entire ecosystem of rules and culture. Ask yourself, is this system designed to have a few winners and a bunch of anxious losers and eventually crater as it feeds on itself? Or is this system designed for all participants to win and to keep winning and expanding the entire ecosystem?

How to Elevate Responsibility in Others

A question I am routinely asked by people who have just learned about The Responsibility Process is "How can I get other people to take responsibility?"

Often after a presentation I'm approached by a successful business owner or corporate boss. They shake my hand, pat me on the shoulder, give me a big grin, and say, "That was an excellent speech on responsibility, Christopher. Now I know why I've always been the responsible one in my business. But Christopher, I'm surrounded by all these people who don't take responsibility. How do I get them to step up?" Can you spot the Lay Blame in this question? The boss was too busy judging others to get my message. He assigns responsibility to himself while saying that those people are the problem. At that moment I am tempted to ask:

- Are these people a problem for you? ("Sure are" he says, confirming the problem in his mind.)

- How did you attract, select, and develop them?

- And for how long have you and the system you oversee been reinforcing them to remain this way?

- And, who could you become for them to show up differently and share responsibility in this system?

But the boss shaking my hand may not be ready to hear that yet.

The fastest way to elevate responsibility in anyone or any group is to demonstrate it yourself—demonstrate your power and ability to create, choose, and attract, both the good and the bad. If your problem is that other people aren't taking ownership, then the sooner you get to and operate from the mental state of Responsibility, the sooner you will model for them how to face this situation, and you may be the type of person they want to follow.

When you adopt a responsibility practice, be Aware you may now be the most responsible person you know in most of your circles. People who practice responsibility at a high level allow others to be who they are instead of invalidating them for not operating from Responsibility.

183

However, people who practice responsibility at a high level do want to be with like-minded others. So two reasons that we want to play win/win games in business and life are because (a) we know we have the integrity to be a successful participant in such environments, and (b) we are more likely to find others there who operate from Responsibility.

Responsibility Practice

Catch yourself thinking *They should take responsibility.* Replace it with *How could I show up in a way that would encourage them to own their situation too?*

Addressing Problems Between

The greatest opportunity to add value in most roles, departments, and organizations goes unrecognized. This is a multitrillion-dollar waste. How does it happen? Let's explore.

Most people agree that the biggest problems are not within roles but between roles, not within teams but between teams, not within departments but between departments, and not within organizations but between organizations. I call these "problems between." Problems between are not assigned to anyone. Why? Because they are between. Most importantly, problems between will remain unresolved until someone chooses to own the problem.

Most of us are experts at spotting problems between because they annoy us. We see them all the time. When we see a problem between, it's easy for us to blame those on the other side of the problem. It's easy to treat the other person as if he were the problem.

"He just isn't doing his job," we blame. We can also Justify our inaction. "It isn't my job to resolve the problem between. I have my job to do."

Problems between will not naturally or magically resolve themselves. Instead, they will continue to cause frustration, expensive coping behaviors, and inaction until someone steps up and owns the problem. Many problems between will require you to recruit others to help you—such as other people on your team, colleagues in other departments, or even sometimes people outside your organization who share responsibility for the problem.

This is an expensive and wasteful by-product of single-point accountability systems. The more your system silos people's focus at any level, the greater the problems between. Conversely, the more your system operates with layers of nested self-directed teams at all levels, the less the problems between you'll create because the self-directed teams own all the impediments that arise.

Responsibility Practice

If you find yourself in a workplace with lots of problems between that no one is owning, you can add a lot of value by expanding your sense of responsibility well beyond your role. Look for potential partners on the other side of a problem between that, if solved, would add tremendous value to the organization. Do a little homework sketching out the problem as a system problem rather than a problem person.

When you approach the person on the other side of the problem, think of her as someone you want to help to win—an ally—regardless of the finger-pointing or other politics that may have come before. Use the concepts of alignment, integration, positive interdependence, and playing a larger game. Here's an outline for your opening message: *Does this problem between hurt you the way it hurts me? Assuming so, I bet to you it looks like I am your problem. And if I was less aware of the real problem, I would probably be blaming you. But I know it is just a problem between. For it to go away, the people being hurt by the problem are going to have to take ownership for it and solve it. I'm willing to do that, and I want your help. What do you think?*

This is an example of demonstrating responsibility as the fastest way to elevate it in others. If you have approached the other person from a tone of 100 percent responsibility, you will likely get her attention and create a substantial opening with her. She'll probably be interested in hearing your ideas about solving the problem.

Addressing Cynicism and Sarcasm

People who are cynical distrust and disparage other people and their motives. Similarly, people who are sarcastic bitterly deride others as well as circumstances. These behaviors are linked to Lay Blame and Justify (i.e., the assumption that the problem is "out there" and deserves to be belittled by me). Here's an example. On my teams, we frequently begin meetings by reporting wins. One of my teammates used cynicism and sarcasm to turn every win into a loss. Listen: "The Acme Company finally paid their outstanding invoice."

When we're cynical, we project on others or external situations instead of taking responsibility. Think about the effects of cynicism. We stay stuck in nonresourceful states longer, because we convince ourselves that the cause of the upset comes from an external source. When we are cynical and sarcastic around others, we lose credibility. We lose the ability to lead them (and ourselves) effectively. However, when we become aware of our cynicism or sarcasm, we have a great opportunity to look within and question our own true intentions.

Here's how I address cynicism and sarcasm within myself. When I become aware of feeling like I am in a position to take a snide swipe at another person or at the world around me, I catch myself and ask, "What do I truly desire?" Sometimes I go on to ask, "Is my Intention in the situation to take Responsibility? Or am I trying to blame or even invalidate someone or some part of my reality for my experience? If so, for how long do I want to give that person the power so I stay a victim?" Second, I make (and express) the intent to free myself quickly. I can take back the power, develop positive intentions, and take positive action.

With teammates, I similarly take Responsibility for creating, choosing, or attracting this situation (i.e., the situation where one of my teammates is critical). In the story I just shared, I asked myself what I wanted. The answer was that I wanted my teammate to actually experience the win.

So one day I asked my teammate to listen to her tone and tell me whether she was reporting a win or a loss. She quickly realized that she was answering the call for wins with a loss. I smiled and asked how long she wanted to remain a loser, especially when she was surrounded by teammates who wanted her to be a winner.

She got it.

Responsibility Practice

It's common to find cynicism and sarcasm in work teams. If you think it is unhealthy and want to turn it around, think of your Intention. What do you want instead of the snarkiness? Confront how you have been colluding with and reinforcing the behavior. Without an audience, the behavior might fade.

Summary

In this chapter we looked at the complex and fuzzy world of shared responsibility. Everywhere in our lives where we share responsibility with others for a larger system of some kind, there are ways we can think and things we can do that can make the relationships and outcomes better (or worse).

To operate successfully and powerfully in shared-responsibility situations, we want to develop Awareness of the dynamics such as alignment and integration. We also want to realize that our own presence in the system—whether it is family, team, coffee club, or traffic—impacts the dynamics of that system. We are a trim tab, able to sway significant leverage with small acts. When we realize this, we set Intentions to lead from Responsibility in ways that invite others to also step up and join us in sharing responsibility. We take Responsibility for our relationships. We realize that Responsibility is leadership, and both are worth sharing throughout the system. We use our integrative power to build relationships of positive interdependence so people feel like they are in the same boat together. We play bigger games, the type of win/win games that invite others to be on our side because we are on theirs. Then it is easy to address problems between and to give no audience to cynicism and sarcasm.

In the next chapter, we move from peer-perspective of sharing responsibility to the perspective of a teacher, coach, parent, or leader developing responsibility in our charges.

8

Developing Responsibility in Others

A potent dynamic exists between practicing responsibility yourself and supporting others in developing their practice. Your ability to teach, coach, and mentor others is governed by your own level of practice. And, your own practice is accelerated when you challenge yourself to teach, coach, and mentor others. So if you want to support others in developing Responsibility, you will want to commit to lifetime mastery, and if you want to accelerate your mastery, commit to teaching and coaching others.

In this section I present four quadrants of lifetime mastery:

- Study

- Demonstrate

- Ask

- Teach

And because of the potentially confusing gulf between "being responsible" and "taking 100 percent responsibility" I also offer two important principles that support the process of teaching or coaching:

1.   Don't go into agreement (i.e., don't validate the coping response).

2.   Stop the responsibility-for-advice transfer.

I end the chapter with my observations on raising responsible children.

Responsibility Practice

When you consider developing Responsibility in others, who comes to mind? Keep them in mind as you read this chapter.

Study The Responsibility Process

The first step to becoming an effective teacher or mentor of Responsibility is committing to study The Responsibility Process and related models—not just book study, but study in application. You don't become a master plumber or electrician through book study but through applied problem solving and application. Mastering Responsibility is the same way.

As you may have gleaned by now in this book, The Responsibility Process and keys look simple and straightforward at first, then as you apply them, the learning curve can get steep quickly. The tools are precise, but general. Problem spaces are messy and specific. Deep emotions are involved. There are so many distinctions that cannot be adequately taught in advance, only learned in real time as you encounter new situations.

Commit to being a student of The Responsibility Process for the rest of your life.

Responsibility Practice

What's your Intention regarding studying Responsibility to the point of mastery?

Demonstrate Responsibility

The second step to lifetime mastery—and thus to teaching or coaching—is to demonstrate Responsibility yourself. As I mentioned in chapter 6 "Lead Yourself First," demonstrating Responsibility is the fastest way to elevate responsibility in anyone or any group.

Talking about "being responsible" and telling others they should take responsibility is for people on a soapbox who want to incite others to do something they themselves aren't doing. Leave the talk to them. Demonstrating Responsibility inspires and enlightens others in ways that simply talking never will.

What if you find yourself in a situation where someone is challenging your authority and what you teach or stand for? It happens to me frequently enough, and sometimes on stage in front of hundreds of others while taking questions. What an opportunity to demonstrate! Demonstrate Responsibility by applying Intention, Awareness, and Confront in real time. Face it now. Ask yourself how you created, chose, or attracted this moment. Then ask yourself what you want about the situation. In my case, I think back and remind myself that vocal proponents of unique ideas attract arrows. "Oh yeah," I say as I smile to myself, "I did ask for this." That helps me face Responsibility. Then, I want to keep breathing and take a moment to get centered. I allow the pause to honor the challenger—the pause says, "Good job, you asked a tough question. I'm gathering my thoughts." Then I realize what an amazing opportunity I have to treat the challenger with empathy and compassion. He isn't bad or wrong. He's simply anxious—maybe even afraid—about what he's hearing from me. I've probably reminded him of some of his problems, and that makes him more anxious. This processing—in real time, in front of an audience—allows me to move from feeling attacked to feeling an opportunity to perhaps reach him, and if not him, then at least inform, intrigue, or inspire others in the room. And so I turn the challenge into an opportunity to demonstrate.

This hasn't always been true. I learned the hard way. In twenty-four years, I've discovered hundreds of ways of demonstrating non-Responsibility in front of people to whom I was ostensibly teaching Responsibility. And each time that happened I—and my subject matter—lost credibility.

Teaching or coaching Responsibility means creating the context of Responsibility. You create that context around you—in the space, the room, with the team, or community—by demonstrating Responsibility yourself, owning your power and ability to create, choose, and attract everything in your reality.

Enough talk. Demonstrate.

Responsibility Practice

Thinking about the people to whom you want to teach Responsibility, what opportunity do they present you to demonstrate Responsibility in real time, under challenging conditions? Are you up for it?

Ask for Responsibility

As we demonstrate Responsibility, we naturally want to surround ourselves with others who operate from Responsibility. We want them to know this gift, this leadership gift, that means so much to us. How much easier would life be if we shared a common language and process for problem solving?

What if we could be human in front of each other, admit we're stuck in a coping strategy, and request help moving to Responsibility? How much more effective could we be? How fulfilling would it be?

Unless you have an agreement with another person to operate from Responsibility, you have no right to expect it. After all, humans are subject to The Responsibility Process, so Lay Blame, Justify, Shame, Obligation, and Quit are all natural emotional coping responses to problems. As I've said in earlier chapters, The Responsibility Process only works when it's self-applied. You can't make anyone take it, not even yourself. You can however, invite it and nurture it.

As a new practitioner of The Responsibility Process, this can drive you batty if you don't know how to handle it. Suddenly, you are the most responsible person you know in most situations. Everywhere you go you see people acting out The Responsibility Process. You see smart, educated, ambitious people unconsciously blaming, justifying, and operating from Shame, Obligation and Quit. You want to shake them, help them, correct them. You want to share what you know!

And there is only one way to begin the conversation. Ask. Ask for Responsibility.

The perfect opportunity is in a new relationship, perhaps a newly formed team. In a new relationship, there is always an opportunity early on to state your interests, and to ask for operating agreements. My favorite operating agreement to request is that we agree to operate from Responsibility. Here's how I do this. I say, "My most important request is that we do our best to operate from Responsibility in our work together, knowing full well that things will go wrong, and that we'll feel like blaming and justifying, yet we will get ourselves back to the mental state of Responsibility, which is the only place we can really solve the problem." Making the request—the ask—as some say, then gives you an opportunity to teach, which is the subject of the next section.

Ongoing relationships can present more challenge in terms of how to ask. After all, you may have cocreated norms of coping, defensiveness, and resistance. It may not be easy or safe to simply ask for Responsibility. Or maybe it will be. Each relationship is unique. This is an opportunity for you to apply the Three Keys to Responsibility. What do you really want most in this relationship? What do you have? How will you change to have the relationship you want?

Responsibility Practice

Think of two or three people or groups that you want to ask to join you in doing your best to operate from Responsibility together. Envision it going well, seeing yourself in your mind's eye knowing just what to say so people feel good about your proposal. If you are having difficulty envisioning it going well, then there is likely something for you to Confront—to learn about yourself. Continue imagining the ask going well until you become Aware of whatever is holding you back.

Teach The Responsibility Process

Asking for Responsibility naturally leads to teaching The Responsibility Process, which offers a number of benefits. First, it opens the conversation about how our minds react to upset, so that we can talk about it rather than deny it. Second, it interrupts the cultural trance and our unexamined programming about whether Responsibility is simply our moral character, or whether it is how we learn and grow (or avoid learning and growing). Third, teaching Responsibility often inspires and intrigues others to begin applying it right away. It's heartwarming when someone approaches you after learning The Responsibility Process and says "Thank you, I needed to hear that today. I've been stuck in a big problem, and you helped me get unstuck."

People vary in their readiness to introduce others to The Responsibility Process. Some people can't wait to share it with family and colleagues. Other's say they want to but just don't feel ready. I've found this is often a little bit of perfectionism, of not feeling good enough yet. These people think they aren't good enough yet to share The Responsibility Process, because they are still subject to it (i.e., they are still blaming, justifying, shaming themselves, etc.). My response is if you have to wait until you are perfect, until nothing ever goes wrong, and you never experience the coping mental states, then you will be waiting forever. In fact, the best way to teach The Responsibility Process to others is to tell stories about your own coping habits. You can do that by giving examples of how you have recently caught yourself in Lay Blame, Justify, Shame, Obligation, Quit, and Responsibility.

And I'll give you an outline with all the teaching points. Just download and print The Responsibility Process poster pdf in full color from ChristopherAvery.com. It's available in nearly thirty languages including Klingon. On the second page of the pdf is a summary of The Responsibility Process and the Three Keys to Responsibility. You can use these to guide you.

Responsibility Practice

Set an Intention to teach Responsibility to someone soon. To whom? When? What examples of your own coping will you use?

Continue the Virtuous Cycle

Teaching The Responsibility Process, like teaching anything, will challenge you to know and understand it better. So teaching Responsibility leads back to the first quadrant: Study. These four quadrants—Study, Demonstrate, Ask, and Teach—comprise a virtuous and expanding cycle. Each quadrant calls on you to take the next step in an iterative, incremental, and evolutionary experience of increasing power, ability, fulfillment, and value.

For many people, The Responsibility Process becomes the most important information they know and have to share about happiness and success. If you are like them, then you may be on this virtuous cycle for the rest of your life—always learning, always demonstrating, always inviting others to try on The Responsibility Process, and always discovering new opportunities to teach.

Enjoy. And thank you for helping to expand its reach.

Responsibility Practice

Intend to catch yourself teaching Responsibility and thinking to yourself, *Wow, I thought I understood this better than I do.* When you do, stop the self-talk and let it go. Correct to teaching and demonstrating the best you know. Then commit to studying about whatever The Responsibility Process is calling you to study. And commit to catching yourself feeling inadequate earlier the next time.

Don't Go into Agreement: Handling the "Yes, But" Trap

As a teacher, coach, or mentor of Responsibility, you invite people to share their upsets with you. And when you are teaching Responsibility, you are reminding people in your audience of areas where they are coping. In a coaching or mentoring situation, we would first have agreements in place that the coach or mentor can ask you about your Intention, Awareness, and Confront to support you in finding the breakthrough. However in a teaching situation, you don't have those agreements in place because the audience isn't yet ready to ask for support or think about the need for such agreements.

So up goes a hand, and the question comes straight from one of the coping mental states. The person says: "But the bus really did run me over, and I spent six months in the hospital and at home recovering. Are you telling me that is my fault?" Or they say, "But I really did break the build causing my team to miss the release and disappoint management and the customer. Are you telling me I shouldn't feel bad?" Or "But I really do have to go to my manager's stupid meetings. Are you saying I don't have to go?"

Be aware that this is a trap. It's a setup. They may not be intending to put you in a gotcha situation, but still they are. It's also a wonderful opportunity to demonstrate Responsibility because someone is going to get gotten. Either the challenger is going to get you, or you are going to get them. They get you by getting you to agree with their point of view in which case they make the point that the coping state is more real than the growth state of Responsibility. Instead, you can get them by compassionately letting them know that you understand where they are coming from, and that perhaps they can take another look at their viewpoint.

The principle is "don't go into agreement with—i.e., don't validate—their coping state." If you do, they win, and you won't be teaching much more about Responsibility that day.

However, if you are willing to stay centered, face this challenging "yes, but," and see it for what it is which is an opportunity for that person to break through a hurt and find some new freedom and choices, then you can take effective action. Pause and breathe, indicating that they asked a good question, and take a moment to check in with yourself. Then figure out how to make them feel 100 percent supported by you. Sincerely say, "Oh, I'm sorry that happened to you." Then challenge them to take another look at where they are coming from. You might say, "May I push back a bit on your question?" They will usually say, "Sure." Then point to a graphic of The Responsibility Process (I always have one around, especially if I'm teaching, and I recommend you do too) and gently ask, "Where on The

Responsibility Process is the feeling state you are describing?" Sometimes they'll call themselves on it and say, "I guess it is Lay Blame" or "I'm in Shame." And you can simply follow with a "Thank you. Yes. And in that mental state can we solve the problem or do we get to keep it and merely cope with it?" And they, and the entire audience, will likely get the lesson about the power of the mental states.

Sometimes, instead of identifying the mental state, someone will say, "I'm somewhere between Obligation and Responsibility." This is the cultural trance at work. They want to identify with being responsible, yet they are feeling trapped or burdened. When this happens I just say, "Look again, there is no between. If you are in Responsibility then you are feeling great, expansive, light, and free. But if you are feeling bad, or burdened, or trapped, you are somewhere else. Which is it?"

As a teacher, coach, or mentor of Responsibility, not only do you get to Confront your own upsets and anxieties, but also you are successful only to the extent that you can Confront (i.e., face calmly and directly) the upsets and anxieties of others. Doing this will dramatically accelerate your practice and mastery.

Responsibility Practice

Meditate on this question and what it means: Are you willing not only to Confront your own fears and anxieties but also the fears and anxieties of others so that you can effectively teach and demonstrate Responsibility?

Stop the Responsibility-for-Advice Transfer

Practicing Responsibility means thinking for yourself. Yet, when we have a problem, we are conditioned to ask, "What should I do?" Teachers and coaches of Responsibility recognize this question as rooted in Shame or Obligation and will resist answering it directly. There are a number of reasons for this. The most important reason is the responsibility-for-advice transfer. Here is how it works. When you tell people what to do, they hand you responsibility for anything about it that goes wrong. It's as clear an exchange as a cash register transaction; the clerk hands you a pack of gum, and you hand the clerk some cash. The difference is that the cash transaction is transparent where the responsibility-for-advice transfer is much less so. It's unconscious.

When you develop sufficient Awareness of this, you will see the transfer happening everywhere. Some people refer to it as the monkey on the back. Ian is a software manager in Edinburgh. One day as he was confronting why he was working so hard as a team leader and being so ineffective, he realized that he was in a vicious pattern with his team. Because he happily gave them advice about every problem, they happily brought every problem to him. Each time, he told them what they should do, and they transferred their monkey-on-the-back to him. They went off and with little commitment tried to implement the advice and failed. And each time they said his advice didn't work. Can you picture poor Ian with all these monkeys on his back? He owned every single problem all by himself, and the team was happy to let him.

Ian made an important realization. His role was not to tell others what to do but to help them think for themselves, learn, and grow. Instead of giving advice, he asked questions. Making sure he didn't receive a transfer of the responsibility, he would ask: "What have you tried?" "What else have you tried?" "What haven't you tried?" "What do you think is the root cause?" If they insisted that he's the expert and that he should just tell them, Ian would reply, "and how I would approach it may not work for you at all because we are different people, different engineers, and solve problems in different ways." And if they still insisted, or if Ian felt truly compelled to give advice, then to keep the transfer of responsibility from happening, he would offer multiple alternatives. Ian would say "Well, if I were in your shoes, I would be thinking about possible solution A, I would be thinking about possible solution B, and I would be thinking about possible solution C. I would also be thinking about possibilities D, E, and F. However I don't know which if any of those would work for you. You are going to have to figure that out for yourself. Let me know how it goes."

One by one, over the course of a very few weeks, Ian's team members woke up, started taking ownership for problems, and Ian got the monkeys off of his back and back onto the team where they belonged. With this freed up time and attention, Ian was able to spend more time with his stakeholders, enabling him to balance their conflicting priorities, get better visibility of new projects, and make sure the team was working on the highest-value items for the company. Both he and the team have been recognized for this by peers and superiors alike.

The lesson is that we give others advice because their anxiety makes us anxious and we want to do something. Stop. Instead Confront the anxiety and be willing to let it simmer a bit while you take Responsibility for keeping the problem's Responsibility where it belongs.

Stop giving advice, not to be mean or to refuse to be helpful or share your wisdom, but to ensure that others are thinking for themselves. And if you do give advice, give multiple alternatives so the other person retains the Responsibility for thinking for himself and making a choice.

Responsibility Practice

Most students of Responsibility sooner or later develop an Awareness of how addicted they are to advice—both asking for it and giving it, solicited or unsolicited. If you develop this Awareness, know that you can use the Catch Sooner game to change this habit. How? Commit to catching yourself in an advice-for-responsibility transfer. Stop, Correct. Let it go. Commit to catch yourself sooner next time.

What About Our Kids?

Nearly every time I teach The Responsibility Process someone asks, "What about my kids?" Others in the room perk up, nod in agreement, and lean in, sharing their interest in wanting to know how to ensure they are raising responsible children. Boy, talk about feelings of ownership! As parents, we so want to do right by our children. It is no wonder this is a top question for people who learn about The Responsibility Process.

To be clear, I usually ask which type of responsibility the questioner is asking about. Do they want to know how to raise good, obedient, smile-like-you-mean-it kids? Or do they want to raise kids who are truly resourceful and happy and who think for themselves in pursuit of results that truly matter? This is a confronting question, of course, and when faced with it directly—at least in my presentations—the response is the latter. Peter Koestenbaum, the corporate philosopher who writes about personal responsibility and leadership, says that a parent's primary polarity is the same as a leader's primary polarity, which is to take 100 percent responsibility for your charges while teaching them that their life is 100 percent their responsibility.[1] By "polarity" Koestenbaum means competing motives. For instance we want to provide safety for our charges, and we also know that they must experience the natural consequences of their choices in order to get feedback and learn.

I don't claim to be a parenting expert, however, I have thought deeply about parenting and The Responsibility Process, because I, too, have wanted to be a worthy father for my children. I've come to one clear first principle for parenting for and from Responsibility: Demonstrate to your children your own humanity through your practice of Responsibility, and your children will learn what you want them to learn. They will learn how to practice responsibility.

They don't need you to drum The Responsibility Process into them, since they came with it installed. Your job is to demonstrate (not preach) how to successfully navigate it.

What do I mean here by "demonstrate your own humanity"? Simply catch yourself in Lay Blame, Justify, Shame, Obligation, or Quit in front of your children, and then complete the Catch Sooner exercise in front of them. Here's an example: You back the car down the drive and run over your child's skateboard. In a fit of a rage about the number of times you have asked that they not leave their things in the drive, added to the fact that you'll now be later to your appointment than you want to be, you carry the broken skateboard inside, demanding to know who left it under the wheel of the car (so that you can hold them to account, of course). Sooner or later, you are going to realize that you are operating from Lay Blame, coping with rather than solving the real problem. You are making your kids your problem. And you are teaching them to handle problems the same way. When you realize it, simply get off of Lay Blame, and work your way to Responsibility as fast as possible, forgive yourself, and figure out how to apologize to them as soon as possible. Later that day your conversation might go something like this: "Children, I apologize to you for my outburst this morning. I'm not very proud of my behavior because I realize I was coming from pure blame, and that's not going to solve anything."

At that moment, you might not know how to do any more problem solving than to simply confess your own humanity and sincerely apologize. If you have forgiven yourself, you don't need to seek their forgiveness (there is often something forced and false about asking, "Do you forgive me?").

Consider what it means to "raise responsible children" from the viewpoint of society's cultural trance versus the lessons of The Responsibility Process. Society's view of responsibility is a confused contortion of Shame, Obligation, Quit, and Responsibility. From this view we say, "Shame on you" without a thought about the conditioning we are reinforcing. We say, "Shut up and do what you're told" with the same lack of consciousness.

Demonstrating your own humanity in front of your kids means applying Intention, Awareness, and Confront to your parenting choices. I remember the time I caught myself on the back patio of our home, a walk-way between our kid's game room and bedrooms, and my home office. One of my boys wanted my attention and just as I was starting to say, "Daddy *has* to work now," I caught myself. At that moment in my mind, I heard what seemed like a thousand echoes of that phrase spoken daily by parents to kids. Wow, talk about a jolt of Awareness. I asked myself, *Do I really want to demonstrate a life of Obligation to my children on a daily basis? Or would I rather let them see me wrestle with and take ownership of the conscious choice to set aside time for work and time to be with them?* The first is fast, easy, and obviously a coping strategy. The second is harder and messier at first but provides far more freedom, power, and choice.

Have lots of compassion, patience, and forgiveness for yourself and your children. Our species has the longest period of socialization of any on the planet. There is a reason they have been entrusted to you for two (or three or four) decades as they learn to become independent in this increasingly complex world. Remember that they are blaming and making excuses not because they are bad or wrong (or don't listen to what you teach) but because they are human. There is nothing wrong with them. They are operating normally.

Don't make them wrong when they demonstrate coping mechanisms, but don't make them right either. Instead find a way to compassionately empathize yet encourage them to take another look at their mental state. If they say, "I have nothing to wear Friday night, my life is ruined!" You—from a position of Responsibility where you realize that you created, chose, and attracted this child and all their coping mechanisms and that you love them completely and will allow them to think for themselves—might respond, "I'm so sorry, Sweetie, and I'm happy to help you problem solve, but committing to be depressed unless you have a constant supply of new clothes is likely going to keep you depressed rather than solve the problem." This is planting the seed that they are in charge of their mental state. Your goal is that you find a way to gently help them take another look at their mental state. Do this well, while maintaining rapport, and they will learn to do it for themselves.

As your child approaches the age when they can grasp concepts and definitions, maybe from six to twelve years old, you can look for opportunities to teach and discuss The Responsibility Process. Keep it short, sweet, and totally supportive—not a lecture when they don't demonstrate Responsibility. Here's an example. Thom, then ten years old, came into my home office in tears midmorning asking to speak to me. So we sat together, and I asked him what was going on. Thom said that he, his older brother, and Mom were walking the dogs. They had a disagreement about something, and Mom and older brother told Thom he was justifying. When Thom protested, they told him to ask Dad what it meant. I pulled a poster of The Responsibility Process off the wall and held it in front of us. I said, "You might recognize that Justify is one of Dad's words. All it means is that when we are upset, sometimes we make up a story about how the problem is bigger than us, and we are powerless to do anything about it. And if we stop telling ourselves that story, we can move up the list, eventually to Responsibility where we can realize that we are bigger than the problem and do something about it.

Thom had stopped crying but was still sad and a little sniffly. He said thank you and left with the poster. Then an amazing thing happened. He came back a couple of hours later and asked if I had a minute. I said, "Sure Thom." He said, "You know what, Dad? Mom and big brother were right, I was justifying." While contrite, I could also see that he was much more present and alive, enjoying the experience of a little more freedom, power, and choice in his life. I said, "Thank you for telling me Thom, and congratulations on your realization."

Responsibility Practice

Which is more important to you, that your charges do what you think is "right" for them even if it makes them miserable, or that they take ownership of their situation and think for themselves?

Summary

In this chapter we looked at Responsibility from the perspective of a developer of people such as a teacher, coach, parent, or leader. We learned the four quadrants of lifetime mastery:

- Study

- Demonstrate

- Ask

- Teach

And we learned that teaching leads back to studying, so the four quadrants comprise a virtuous cycle that can support you for the rest of your life

We learned the principle of "don't go into agreement" when someone is coping. And we explored how to apply that principle when you are teaching Responsibility and get challenged by someone from a coping state.

Stopping the responsibility-for-advice transfer can keep the monkey of Responsibility where it can do the most good.

And we learned that parents who practice responsibility don't need to worry about raising responsible kids.

In the next chapter, we'll consider how leaders of organizations can create the organization of choice.

9

Leading the Organization
of Choice

This chapter is for the general manager who wants to capture hearts and minds with The Responsibility Process and create a flourishing organization where people experience personal freedom, choice, and power while producing results that matter. It can be any type of organization—business, nonprofit, school, church, anything. By "general manager" I mean someone in a position with the autonomy to create and hold a context for others.

The chapter starts with a success case I was fortunate to witness and ends with a five-step culture-building pattern I've seen in leaders who practice responsibility while also developing it in others. This pattern offers a crucial missing link for bridging Responsibility and accountability.

Setting the Context for Responsibility

Roman (not his real name, and I'll tell you why later), a successful entrepreneur and finance executive, invested in an existing middle-market business—Metal Tank Corporation (a made-up name)—taking the CFO role with expectations to progress to COO and then to CEO over three years. During those three years, Roman saw how his CEO played favorites by protecting one executive's unethical behavior, keeping other key people in the dark, and spending the organization's money lavishly on himself as a show of privilege. So much dysfunction cascaded from this behavior at the top that Roman wondered how the company managed to remain in business.

Metal Tank Corporation's headquarters had the usual setup of a large manufacturing plant occupying most of a city block, with office space at the front. In that office space, the CEO suite, built by the current longtime CEO, occupied almost half of the total space for offices. Roman's first major action as CEO was to dismantle that CEO suite. In its place he expanded and updated offices and meeting rooms for the office staff. For himself, Roman took one of the half-dozen directors' offices, each just big enough for a built-in desk on one wall and a small meeting table for four. This executive action caused a stir among the staff. They had difficulty imagining that Roman was not taking advantage of the CEO suite privilege he had "earned." But Roman did not do it to cause a stir. He did it to right a longstanding wrong, to better equip the people operating the business on whom he relied, and to signal what was important to him.

Roman prioritized his time across running the business and systematically improving all aspects of the business. He adopted Jim Collins' *Good to Great* model of visionary companies[1] as his guide. Then Roman engaged his leadership team to rework Metal Tank's statements of purpose, values, vision, and mission. Roman also introduced The Responsibility Process to his leadership team, explained what an important personal practice it was for him, and invited them to study and practice it with him.

Gradually The Responsibility Process became a core organizing principle and shared language for that leadership team.

Together the leadership team redefined how the company viewed its customers. Previously, customers had been seen as crisis-producing problems the company was obliged to react to and placate. Of course Roman and his team could see that the crisis-producing problems were not "out there" but rather in the way Metal Tank's leadership viewed and manipulated customers and employees. With Roman's leadership team, customers are seen as important stakeholders deserving to be served. Similarly the leadership team changed its view of employees from problems to be managed to stakeholders in the business to be cared about and included.

These changes reveal a gradually expanding practice of personal and shared responsibility in everyday conversations, decisions, and operations. The changes also reveal expanding freedom, choice, and power while also producing results that matter. Little by little Metal Tank retained more accounts and captured new business. Both the retained business and new accounts were more profitable due to the improving operations.

One of Roman's proudest accomplishments happened as a by-product of caring about people's freedom, choice, and power. Labor relations improved dramatically, and union grievances declined to near zero. Why? As the business changed how it viewed customers and its own people, it worked more closely with the factory labor to improve processes, safety, and the quality of life in the factory. Indeed, soon after the offices were remodeled, the company invested in making the factory safer, quieter, brighter, and cleaner. Metal Tank invested in Lean concepts to reorganize the factory floor for better flow. Roman did not do these things as a strategy to reduce grievances. He did them to demonstrate Responsibility for the business and its stakeholders, and to increase personal freedom, choice, and power. He did it to produce results that matter.

At least twice Metal Tank shut down the factory for an hour, assembled all the workers on the shift—about one hundred of them—in a cleared out staging area of the factory, set up a portable sound system, and brought me in to give a talk on The Responsibility Process. The factory workers occupied the limited seating. The office staff filled in what was left. The entire leadership team stood indicating their gratitude for the factory employees and their pride in sharing this message with them. They also set up a video link to satellite offices in other parts of the country and the world. Roman introduced me and told the factory workers that today's message about The Responsibility Process was not a new policy, strategy, or program. It was simply a gift of information he and other leaders found useful in their lives, work, and relationships, and wanted to share.

On my second trip to present at the factory, Roman introduced me to a huge man with tattoos of a local Puerto Rican gang covering the exposed areas of his arms, neck, and shaved head. Before Roman's tenure as CEO, this man was dour and a significant source of grievances. On this day he smiled, high-fived Roman, and told me about how he had The Responsibility Process poster at his workbench and, more importantly, on his refrigerator at home where he and his wife discussed it together and with their children.

Roman's director of offshore manufacturing translated The Responsibility Process poster into languages spoken in those locations. Together they used it as a core organizing tool and a shared language to increase openness, clarity, trust, problem ownership, and shared responsibility as stakeholders in each other's businesses.

As the everyday practice of Responsibility spread from the general manger to the leadership team and then to staff, to the factory workers, and even to suppliers and customers, people felt more free and at choice, they were happier at work, revenues grew, profit margins grew, and the company's valuation grew making Roman's investment a good one.

Responsibility Practice

Consider how one person in a manager position in any organization can create and hold a context for Responsibility that successfully invites scores of others to step into and embrace that context of Responsibility. Consider his Intention, Awareness, and Confront. Consider how she naturally deploys the Catch Sooner game.

Metal Tank Corporation Epilogue

I promised to tell you why I don't use the real names for Roman or Metal Tank Corporation. Metal Tank Corporation's major investor took advantage of Roman's excellent results and sold his shares to a new investor at a substantial profit. The new majority owner showed more interest in financial statements than in people, purpose, and values. With control of the board, the new investors reduced Roman's autonomy by pushing him for better short-term financials, not through people and continuous improvements, but through shortcuts. They pushed him to employ harsh tactics with suppliers, raise prices to customers, and reduce operating expenses thus crippling what staff could get done. During this time, Roman confided to me that his job had gone from being the best he had ever had to the worst. Even a CEO can have a destructive boss. After a year, the board asked Roman to resign or be fired. The reason I don't use the real names for Roman and the company is because Roman's severance agreement includes a punitive nondisclosure clause.

Responsibility Practice

Speculate on what happened to Metal Tank's account retention, new customer acquisition, market share, revenues, profitability, employee morale, and union relations after Roman left.

Responsibility First, Then Accountability

In the organization of choice, the culture focuses first on personal responsibility and then on role accountability. I call this Responsibility *over* accountability. When a leader and organization values personal responsibility over role accountability, they get much higher levels of self-leadership, self-management, personal responsibility and shared responsibility throughout the system. They get a system overflowing with leadership at all levels. They get happy (and joyous) people and high performance. And few people ever need to be called to account.

Instead of needing status meetings and performance management meetings to inquire about why people are failing, people participate in team meetings, feedback loops, stand ups, and retrospectives where they are responding to the thousand little things that they can correct and improve. They are experiencing freedom, choice, and power.

You can easily diagnose and monitor any workplace to assess this for yourself. On the one hand, organizations that promote accountability systems over personal responsibility tend toward more complicated and onerous performance management systems to gain a false sense of control over the system. The greater the presence of such systems, the less Responsibility will be practiced throughout the organization. On the other hand, organizations that promote personal responsibility over accountability tend toward lightweight, simple, and barely sufficient performance management systems. Why? Because people in such an organization do not need to be "held to account" to perform highly.

So develop your Intention to put responsibility over accountability and get started. You will likely become highly aware of the controlling nature of your performance management systems. Most managers I consult who came to this realization found a way to modify their own use of the mandated tools to lead from and for Responsibility. You probably can too until such time as you can change the systems. The main thing to Confront is how to honor Responsibility over accountability in everyday situations. Practicing the basics presented in this book will support you. The tool in the next section will supercharge you as a leader and culture builder.

Responsibility Practice

Do you agree that most organizations put "holding others to account" ahead of "practicing responsibility"? Assuming so, why do you think that is the case? More pointedly, how might you be complicit?

The Five-Step Culture-Building Bridge from Responsibility to Accountability

By this point, you may be wondering if there is a bridge from Responsibility to accountability. Good question. The answer is yes, there is. If we cannot connect feelings of ownership with performance expectations, then we can't lead and manage effectively. The bridge must connect two or more people or groups with performance expectations of each other, to the feelings of ownership in each. The pattern naturally unfolds in five steps:

1. Am I operating from Responsibility?

2. Do I know what I want?

3. Have I asked for what I want?

4. Do I have agreement for what I asked for?

5. If 1–4 are "Yes," then call to account.

People practicing responsibility will only move to the next step if they can honestly answer yes to that step.[2] Let's examine each step.

1. Am I Operating from Responsibility?

Practicing Responsibility means asking yourself, *How did I create, choose, or attract this?* when facing unwanted results. For the leader of any organization, this means at some level you assume 100 percent responsibility for all causes and effects. If you don't, you are denying your ability to lead. When you do, you refuse to Lay Blame or Justify—behaviors that are far too common in hierarchical leaders. You know Shame and Obligation produce poor results. So you get to ask yourself, *What part of these unsatisfactory results are mine to own?* This of course is Confront at work as you explore your thoughts looking for insights about how to lead your organization to results that matter.

In Roman's case, he saw the years of dysfunctional leadership and culture as the thing he most wanted to change in order to produce results that mattered. He did not create the dysfunction. He did attract it since he invested in the company, and he did choose it since he also took a leadership role. So when he became CEO, he accepted 100 percent responsibility for the dysfunction and set out to change it. He could have said, "I inherited this, there's nothing I can do." But he did not. Instead he said, "I chose this."

When you get yourself into the mental state of Responsibility, it leads naturally to asking yourself, *What do I want to be different so that we can get a better result?*

2. Do I Know What I Want?

Intention is the first Key to Responsibility and to leadership. Asking yourself what you want about a situation is the natural next step after checking to see that you are responding from Responsibility. If you aren't crystal clear about what you want, you can't effectively communicate direction.

As we discovered earlier in the book, knowing what you want can be much more Confronting than lashing out at people for results you don't want—a tactic employed by too many supposed leaders. Leaders practicing responsibility seek personal clarity about what they do want before they address others associated with the problem. Clarity about what they want might lead the leader to new Awareness about his or her own behavior. Or it might mean asking others to change.

Following our example of Roman, he knew that he wanted a senior leadership team committed to a shared purpose, vision, values, and mission. He also knew that he wanted The Responsibility Process as a shared organizing principle and shared language. The next thing to do was to ask his senior leaders for what he wanted.

3. Have I Asked for What I Want?

How quickly and easily we judge others because we know what *they should* have done. Such judgment isn't going to change what they did. It is going to keep us from operating in Responsibility, and if we let our judgment loose on them, they likely won't be operating in Responsibility. Instead, the leader who practices Responsibility realizes that most people are doing the best they know how at the time. The leader also knows that just because he or she knows what others should do or think does not mean that it has been effectively asked for or agreed to.

Making a request can be the beginning of a new relationship. It can mean asking for help or offering help, each of which is a move from independence to interdependence, or teamwork. Asking for what you want from other people also preserves their choice, the choice to say yes as opposed to the obligation to say it.

Within days of Roman's appointment as CEO, he approached each of the other senior leaders and initiated a conversation about working together as the leadership team to craft a new and aligned sense of purpose and vision for Metal Tank Corporation and for themselves as a team. Roman knew that to produce the results he wanted, he would benefit from having a highly aligned and inspired senior leadership team operating from choice.

Now, the exploration and negotiation toward agreement was under way.

4. Do I Have Agreement for What I Asked For?

Leaders who operate from Responsibility enjoy the feelings of freedom, choice, and power that come along with it. They also want others to experience the same. And the way to do that is to lead in such a way that preserves other's choices and the responsibility for those choices. Such leaders are keenly aware that yes is only meaningful in a relationship if no is also. Practicing Responsibility means identifying areas and opportunities for true agreement where each party freely chooses yes. If you use authority to command another into agreement, that person won't be operating from Responsibility. What you get isn't agreement. At best, you get Obligation and compliance as long as you can monitor it.

Roman and the leadership team invested considerable time together reaching agreement on purpose, vision, values, and mission. Then they invested more time together turning the ideology into strategy and tactics for every part of the business. Seldom did any of the leadership team need to think twice about whether another member of the team would follow through with what they had agreed.

5. If 1–4 Are "Yes," Then Call to Account

The leader operating from Responsibility can, with full integrity, call other people to account for their actions or choices. Why? Because the leader has done the groundwork to establish where the breakdown actually occurred.

On one of my visits to Metal Tank Corporation after an absence of nearly a year, I noticed that George, the longtime VP of sales, was no longer with the company. I asked Roman what happened, and he responded, "Some of the other members of the leadership team and I noticed a change in George. He was violating multiple team operating agreements that he had followed previously. George wasn't interested in meeting with us as a team, had lots of excuses about why he couldn't, and began making decisions and taking actions that were counter to the productive norms our executive team had established. He also wasn't meeting his numbers and refused our help.

"For about a month I observed his behavior to try to understand what was going on. I was concerned for George. I also realized that I did not want this situation to continue for long. I wanted to help George either get realigned with us or find a better place for his talents. So I met with him privately and shared my observations and concerns both for the company and for him. I asked if he was okay. I asked if something was going on in his life we should know about so that we could support him. George said everything was fine in his personal life. About his new behaviors, he said he wanted to operate independently from the rest of the leadershp team to do his job. He said he could simply report to me rather than coordinate with the larger leadership team, which included the COO, the CFO, and the VP for offshore manufacturing—all important partners for the sales VP. I listened and asked questions to make sure I understood his proposal. What he was demonstrating and insisting on was a significant departure from the high-performing leadership team we had enjoyed for a number of years.

I asked if there was any middle ground. He said, 'No.' At that point, it became clear to me that George was no longer a fit for how our leadership team worked, and I suggested he think about that. He balked. We agreed to a twenty-four hour cooling off period. When we spoke the next day, he was even more adamant and made new demands to run the sales organization completely independently from the leadership team. I declined and asked for his resignation."

In taking this action Roman progressed naturally and step-by-step across the bridge from Responsibility to accountability. He continually checked to make sure that he was operating from Responsibility (Step 1). He knew what he wanted (Step 2), a cohesive high-performing leadership team that modeled cross-functional and silo-busting leadership through-out the organization. He asked George for what he wanted (Step 3) which was a team-based approach to leadership in the organization. He pursued agreement for what he wanted (Step 4) but did not receive it. He tried multiple approaches to find agreement but did not. Only then did he hold George to account (Step 5), which in this case resulted in separation from the role and from employment. Most acts of holding another to account need not be so severe. This was an illustrative case of a significant and puzzling change in behavior, philosophy, and results that defied an amicable resolution.

Responsibility Practice

The five steps to accountability reveal a progressive set of Intentions, Awarenesses, and Confronts that a practitioner of Responsibility steps through on the way to holding another to account. Consider how you call others to account. How can these five steps play out for you?

Summary

In this chapter, we showed how a general manager with sufficient autonomy can create and hold a context for Responsibility that allows an organization to grow and flourish. When this happens, you get an organization of choice. The case of Roman and Metal Tank Corporation showed how a general manager practicing responsibility can transform an organization. The case also showed us how the context can change again when that general manager no longer has the autonomy to create and hold the context or when the general manager is replaced.

We then looked at the essential difference in an organization of choice—that the leadership and then the people demonstrate that they value the practice of personal responsibility over role accountability. This then reveals a culture-building pattern where people practicing responsibility have a natural series of Intentions, Awarenesses, and Confronts that they go through before they hold another person to account.

In the concluding chapter, we look at a set of principles that emerge along the road to mastery.

Conclusion
On the Road to Mastery

To bring this book to conclusion, this chapter revisits and summarizes core principles, truths, and practices that arise again and again as reminders or signposts in conversations about Responsibility among colleagues, students, and teachers. If you intend to master Responsibility, you will want to turn to these signposts frequently.

When You Master Responsibility, You Master Your Life

When you have used the tools in this book to routinely find, address, and solve the real problem, then you will create more and more alignment with your core being, beliefs, values, and purpose. You will be more free, powerful, and at choice. You will have more of what you want and you will want what you have—not in a selfish way, but in a fulfilling and generous way. You will own your power and ability to create, choose, and attract the reality you desire.

It is not easy. I never promised it would be. Confronting anxieties is hard. It is, however, straightforward. The tools are precise and actionable. They work for anybody and everybody who wants change, who wants to lead themselves or others, and who wants to experience the ultimate benefits of taking ownership of life.

When you think someone or something else is responsible for your problems and their solutions, that thought is the first problem you must solve. As we learned in the early chapters, you will never resolve a problem that you aren't owning 100 percent. Even though it may appear that the problem is "out there," it is defined "in here" (i.e., in the mind). That's where the anxiety is. So that is where the resolution needs to happen.

The Responsibility Process, the Three Keys to Responsibility, and the Catch Sooner Game are the tools you use to find and solve the real problem over and over and over again for life.

The Responsibility Process only works when it's self-applied. The Responsibility Process is not a management tool. It backfires when we use it as a weapon to Lay Blame on others.

The Responsibility Process is a tool for self-leadership, the most potent tool I know. It is also all natural so it is already "installed" for use. In fact, whether or not you choose to practice responsibility consciously, The Responsibility Process is already at work, all day, every day, every time something goes wrong. Executives ask me, "Christopher, do you think The Responsibility Process will work in my company?" I respond by saying it's already at work full-time. The more important question is "How's it working? Do your leadership and cultural norms around problems and frustrations lead people to cope or to grow?"

To access The Responsibility Process, use the three keys of Intention, Awareness, and Confront, as described in chapter 4 "The Three Keys to Responsibility." Each of these is a mental power with which you were born and can develop with application and practice.

This principle is routinely violated by peer leaders (chapter 7 "Sharing Responsibility, Sharing Leadership"), developers of people (the subject of chapter 8 "Developing Responsibility in Others"), and organizational leaders (chapter 9 "Leading the Organization of Choice"). All leadership starts with self-leadership. If you want others to operate from Responsibility, then you must also.

Below the line we talk about problems; above the line we solve them. As we learned in chapter 7, "Sharing Responsibility, Sharing Leadership," kibitzing, complaining, sniping, and cynicism are all fabulous signs that we are coping with rather than owning and addressing problems. These negative stances promote terminal normality and ordinariness. Want extraordinary? As we learned in chapter 5 "The Catch Sooner Game," catch yourself talking about any problem, change by asking yourself what you really want about it, have compassion for self, and then vow to catch yourself sooner next time.

Good People Routinely Avoid Taking Responsibility

In the introduction we looked at the vast gap between being responsible and taking 100 percent responsibility. We learned that most people are more focused on being good, responsible members of society than on taking 100 percent responsibility. And in chapter 3 "The Responsibility Process," we learned how good, smart, generally responsible people, naturally avoid owning problems. It's how we cope when we don't know how to learn. We are conditioned to feel bad about a problem or to do what we are supposed to even if we don't like it, instead of growing and thinking for ourselves.

There are too many books and articles written about how to cope. We don't need better coping strategies, we need breakthrough strategies for growth.

Responsibility isn't my character, it is what I practice. Society deems us responsible if we are good citizens. The Responsibility Process and related tools described in chapters 3, 4, and 5, provide a different lens—Responsibility is not *who* I am, it is *what* I practice.

My desire for you and others is that you, too, see Responsibility not as who you are but as what you practice. I know you can practice and master Responsibility to shape your life, relationships, and work in the direction that you want.

We are fully equipped to both take and avoid responsibility. Our society's cultural trance wants us to believe that some people have it—responsibility that is—and others don't. The Responsibility Process suggests a different lens. It shows that we are all subject to natural thoughts about avoiding Responsibility and about taking it. Practicing Responsibility simply means accepting our humanity (in terms of our natural coping thoughts), noticing those thoughts, and choosing to operate instead from Responsibility.

We are more powerful and able than we usually give ourselves credit for. This is one of my favorite truths and a major theme that runs throughout every chapter of this book. I know that I am more powerful and able than I usually give myself credit for.

Here's why I know this. In our coping states, we cannot see how we could have possibly created, chosen, or attracted the problem that upsets us, so we don't give ourselves the credit we are due (for creating, choosing, or attracting what we don't like and don't want). We deny Responsibility for the problem and unconsciously presume the problem is more powerful than we are.

When we remind ourselves that we can be more powerful than any problem, then we embrace both the problem and our humanity. We are both humbled and strong. We realize we can generate new choices and newfound freedoms and power.

We aren't bad or wrong for avoiding responsibility; we are simply and gloriously human. When we realize that there is nothing wrong with us—or them—for having thoughts of Lay Blame, Justify, Shame, Obligation, and Quit, and that we are functioning perfectly as wonderful, fragile, and brilliant humans, then we can start to solve the true problems. This realization, established early in the book, can induce healing thoughts of compassion, humility, and freedom that can release us to new learning and growth.

Think of someone you are judging harshly at the moment. It might even be yourself. Now consider this: What if there is nothing wrong with them (or you)? What if they (or you) are merely human, experiencing the natural mental thought patterns that all humans experience? Does considering this change your thoughts about how to handle the situation?

Smarter people just make up better stories. You might think that smart, educated, accomplished people would recognize the folly of Lay Blame, Justify, Shame, and Obligation and naturally practice responsibility at higher levels than those who are less intelligent, educated, or accomplished. They don't. Why? Because Responsibility is not about intelligence or traditional thinking tools. Instead it is about our response to anxiety. Smarter people (and those of status and authority) simply contrive better and more convincing stories about why their problems are more powerful than they are.

To test this for yourself, listen for the executive, celebrity, or politician version of "the dog ate my homework." It will be many times longer than five words and contain dramatic and convincing "fact" and detail.

Then remember, there is nothing wrong with those individuals, they are simply coping with a problem they don't yet know how to own.

Nothing Real Happens Until Someone Takes Ownership of a Problem

There is so much talk about responsibility and accountability. If you are listening, you hear it many times a day, from advertisers, politicians, pundits, experts, and colleagues. Unfortunately, 99.99 percent of it is just talk, not actual demonstration. Until someone truly takes ownership, we will be stuck talking about problems and nothing valuable will happen.

Personal responsibility always trumps role accountability. This was the subject of chapter 2 "Responsibility ≠ Accountability." We can make agreements, assign accountabilities, and hold people obligated, all in the name of expected results. However, our real outcomes depend on how we and others respond when things don't go as planned—and things never go as planned. When we focus on role accountability over personal responsibility, we get unhappy people and mediocre performance. When we lead from and for personal responsibility over role accountability, we get happy people and miraculous performance.

To put this principle to work, consider expanding your sense of Responsibility a little wider, bit by bit, in all areas of your life. I don't mean expand your sense of Shame, as in feeling bad for things not done or not going well, nor your sense of Obligation, as in having to take on more duties. I mean expand your willingness to respond, to integrate with, rather than separate from, your environment. At work this could mean holding the larger purpose and vision so you are playing a bigger game and focusing on results that truly matter. In other areas of your life it means focusing on what you truly want to be, to do, and to have, instead of on what the cultural trance expects of you.

People naturally take Responsibility for what interests and inspires them. In chapter 6 "Lead Yourself First," we looked at relearning how to want, with the idea that our cultural trance grooms us to do what we are supposed to do instead of what truly interests us and releases our genius. We also looked at the characteristics of good goals, which clarify Intention, focus attention, remove obligation, and generate energy. When people are naturally inspired in their pursuits, they tend to cope less and grow more. When we are in pursuit of what we truly want, rather than what society convinces us we should want, then Responsibility comes more easily and naturally.

We can easily be incentivized to do not what truly inspires us but what provides temporary safety, security, a paycheck, or approval perhaps. And we can always incentivize employees, customers, suppliers, and others (like students, children, and other charges) to do what they don't really want to do. But it is a short-term drug that requires frequent doses and leads to a controlling dependency in which the subject feels powerless and trapped in a plush cell. Some people call this leadership. Others call it manipulation. In either case, it is a short-tem gain at the great unseen expense of lack of purpose, passion, and the associated ability to respond. Good goals energize and remove obligation.

To apply this concept, ask yourself if who you are and what you are pursuing inspires you. If the answer is anything less than "Hell Yes," then create an Intention to find a more inspiring goal in life or at work.

To apply this in a leadership situation with others, consider looking together for a larger and more compelling purpose and vision—even in your present work—that would make it more fun and interesting to get out of bed every day and be energized about your team.

Leaders make themselves by how they repeatedly step up and respond to problems. The debate about whether leaders are born or made is over, a point we made in chapter 7 "Sharing Responsibility,

Sharing Leadership." Leadership is innate in all of us as evidenced by The Responsibility Process. We are all born with the ability to step up to problems and opportunities that are larger than we are, but we don't all develop that ability.

We can develop our innate leadership through the repeated practice of Intention, Awareness, and Confront against ever greater challenges. In doing so, we grow in our ability to handle things, we grow in our belief in ourself, and we grow in our Intentions, our inspiration, and our pursuit of results that matter. Others follow when our vision and purpose is both truly worthy and larger than we can accomplish by ourselves.

To apply this notion, simply take the next step. What problem or opportunity exists right now, in a field or domain that interests you, that you truly want to do something about? This world has lots and lots of problems—messes even—that are waiting for someone to step up and take ownership. What's the next one for you?

And to apply this as a leader or developer of others, who would you be if you were allowing your charges or colleagues to be inspired and step up to a problem or opportunity? How can you create and hold a context for safety and freedom that encourages people to do so?

Every Upset Is an Opportunity to Learn

Like it or not, we define what does and does not upset us. The illusion is that the problem is "out there." This is a function of *attribution*, the psychological principle we learned in chapter 1 "What Is Personal Responsibility?" The source of the real problem is our internal conflict between what we want and what we have. The problem can only be addressed successfully at its source. If we cope with the problem, we don't learn and we get to keep the problem. Only by owning it can we grow to overcome the problem.

Responsibility is about what we think and do when things go wrong. This is another theme that runs through every chapter of this book. Denial, Lay Blame, Justify, Shame, and Quit are all definitions in use for the word *responsibility*. We say:

- "It's his responsibility; he ignored the warnings." (In context, "responsibility" implies the actor operated from Denial.)

- "She's responsible for the accident." (Here, "responsible" implies Lay Blame.)

- A traffic jam was responsible for the team missing its competition. (In context, "responsible" implies Justify.)

- He finally took responsibility for bankrupting the company. (Here, "responsibility" implies Shame.)

- He stepped up to his responsibility to put in the overtime. (In context, "responsibility" implies Obligation.)

- He did the responsible thing and gave up on his dream to be a musician. (Here, "responsibile" implies Quit.)

The Responsibility Process helps us accurately understand and penetrate these perceptions of cause and effect. We redefine the coping states for what they are. And we redefine Responsibility to mean truly owning our power and our ability to create, choose, and attract.

We're always creating, choosing, and attracting our reality. We just aren't always owning it, especially when we don't want what we have.

The point of power is in the present. Our angst, great or small, sends our minds time traveling to the past and future. We revisit, fixate on, guilt-trip ourselves or others, and complain about the past, which, of course, we cannot change. Or, we worry about the future, invent false risks or inflate real ones, and set out to solve problems that we don't currently have and may never have. When we think this way, we aren't in the now, the present, because our stressors are taking us to the past (guilt) and to the future (worry) where we are powerless. Now is the perfect moment, the only moment, to accept and develop your gifts and talents. Find your center—who you are, your core beliefs, values, and principles—breathe, and demonstrate Responsibility.

Continually Discover and Focus On What You Want

Intention is the first key to Responsibility. If you don't want to operate from Responsibility, the other keys don't matter. As a sentient being, you have unique interests and gifts, and you have the right to pursue and enjoy them.

Allow yourself to want. So many well-intentioned parents and teachers developed and exercised our brains through our need for their approval while shutting out our hearts. We learned to do what they said. We discovered the safe path and held on tight while simultaneously feeling trapped by it. We learned not to want—to invalidate our wants. We learn not to trust our wants. If we can't trust ourselves and each other to feel, to want, to desire, to dream, and to be inspired, then we will never pursue what truly matters.

So we get to relearn how to want. We get to take responsibility for our programming and choose to recondition ourselves. As we do this, we can discover what's most important for us to experience in abundance on a daily basis. As we get our biggest wants in order, then our smaller wants can take their place.

Not choosing is a choice. So much has been determined or decided for you by your genes and the conditioning of your environment. Claim your freedom by demanding to choose what you want to experience in life, work, and relationships.

Choices have consequences. That's why we have the concept of responsibility—the perception of cause and effect. Understanding and accepting the complexities of our choices and consequences brings us great fulfillment and joy. When we produce a consequence we don't want, we can either cope with the problem or we can examine our role in producing the consequence and adjust how we make choices in the future. Sometimes a client will ask me, "Christopher, if I did *X*, would that be Responsible?" And I say, "I don't know, but here's how you can tell. If you do *X* are you willing to have—to own—any and all the consequences? If yes, then you would be operating from Responsibility."

Check In and Notice Your Point of View

Awareness is the second key to Responsibility and the key to change. Perspective is extremely valuable.

Resistance—refusing to accept—creates anxiety and saps energy. Our coping mind is exceptional in its ability to construct and hold force fields against everything we don't like and think is wrong with life, other people, and the world. But this makes us critical, cynical, arrogant, trapped, powerless, and tired. Dropping the resistance—letting go—and seeing things as they are doesn't mean we like them or choose them. It means we have the power to face them and change them.

Everything we resist persists. Responsibility masters don't fight against what they don't like and don't want. Doing so creates, chooses, and attracts more of it. Instead, responsibility masters identify what they do want and move toward it. As you learn and practice The Responsibility Process, if you get annoyed and angry at yourself for laying blame, justifying, etc., then you will actually experience it more than if you accept it as part of being human and then commit to aligning your intentions toward Responsibility.

What we attend to grows. If you are in traffic and focus on how rude and uncaring other drivers are, you will see more and more of it. If instead you focus on how well you can serve and flow with other drivers around you, you will find more opportunities. If you focus on what is lacking in your paycheck, your relationship, or in yourself, you will brainstorm long and compelling lists of scarcity and hardship. If instead you focus on wins, you will experience more of what you want in abundance.

Clarity leads to power. Confusion and uncertainty keep us stuck. When we see things clearly—as they are—we trust ourselves. This is the source of personal power. The more we practice responsibility, the more we see things as they are and integrate them with our reality.

When We Confront a Problem, We Begin to Solve It

The third key to Responsibility is Confront, or the ability to face something. It shows us how easily we shy away from or avoid problems or even just uncertainty.

Problems exist. There is no life without struggle. Advertisers want you to believe that with enough money you can buy ease and convenience. That's not true. When a big societal problem, or a big engineering problem, or some other big problem inspires you, then confronting it and operating from Responsibility is easy. It is play, not work. The other problems we have, the ones that don't inspire us? We can only solve them by facing them.

Learning happens in no time. It's not learning that takes time. Avoiding means not learning. And it means keeping the problem. Only by confronting the problem and wading in will we begin to learn how to solve it.

For Things to Change, First I Must Change

When we want things outside of us to change to make us happy, we are powerless to make that happen. When we change the way we look at things—by taking ownership of the problem—then the things we look at change. Then we become powerful enough to lead the change we want to see.

When we operate from Responsibility, we experience many benefits:

- We have the opportunity to grow and not simply cope with problems.

- We can capture and experience the three ultimate benefits: freedom, power, and choice.

Feeling free, powerful, and at choice means so much for us, our families, teams, and organizations, and it offers:

- a happy, fulfilling life,

- wonderful relationships,

- a great job,

- and more.

As a student and teacher of The Responsibility Process for twenty-five years, I've had the great fortune of working with individuals like you who strive for mastery.

For you, I want:

- clarity of mind,

- fulfillment,

- a low-stress life,

- resourcefulness,

- high engagement,

- wonderful relationships,

- satisfying work,

- a desire to teach others about The Responsibility Process, and of course,

- The Responsibility Process' ultimate benefits: freedom, power, and choice.

I hope you embrace the opportunity that you have right now for personal change and transformation. Remember: The upset is mine. For things to change; first, I must change.

To be more resourceful and to take shared ownership of problems, don't wait for the other person, take the first steps toward operating from a position of Responsibility more often.

I want you to accept change and not tolerate negative, limiting, coping emotions. Adjust the way you feel about situations when you experience upsets or anxiety. Talk to others about The Responsibility Process. Don't beat yourself up for being human, and celebrate wins! Remember—a win is any Intention that's met.

Thank you for reading this book and sharing this journey. You have a gift to apply to your own life and to share with others. I hope that it benefits you, your teams, and your organizations. Keep your momentum—make this a sustainable change and strive for continued mastery.

Keep at it. You deserve a more productive way to live and lead.

Notes

Introduction:
A More Productive Way to Live and Lead

1. Haskins, R., "The Sequence of Personal Responsibility,"
   Brookings, July 2009, http://www.brookings.edu/research/
   articles/2009/07/09-responsibility-haskins.

2. Canfield & Switzer, 2004; Covey, 1990; Goldsmith, 2013; Hill,
   1937; Peale, 1952; Robbins, 1992; Schuller, 1984.

3. Sivers, 2011. Reprinted with permission.

4. Sivers, D. "Everything Is My Fault." Blog, December 9, 2012.
   http://sivers.org/my-fault. Reprinted with permission.

Chapter 1:
What Is Personal Responsibility?

1. "Personal Responsibility and Work Opportunity Act," Wikipedia,
   last modified May 26, 2016, http://en.wikipedia.org/wiki/
   Personal_Responsibility_and_Work_Opportunity_Act.

2. These quotes appear across the Internet. I have not found original
   sources.

3. Attributed to Epictetus across the Internet (e.g., http://www.brainyquote.com/quotes/quotes/e/epictetus149126.html). An original citation cannot be found. Since the phrase represents a well-known portion of the Stoic philosophy, it is probable that it came from an unavailable translation of Epictetus.

4. Homer, *The Odyssey*, Book 1, The Literature Network, http://www.online-literature.com/homer/odyssey/1/.

5. "Attribution (psychology)," Wikipedia, last modified March 28, 2016, https://en.wikipedia.org/wiki/Attribution_(psychology).

6. Malle, 2004.

7. Bandura, 1997.

8. Ibid.

9. Plato, 2009.

10. Ruble R., "Determinism vs Free Will," *JASA* 28, June 1976, http://asa3.org/ASA/PSCF/1976/JASA6-76Rubble.html.

11. Durant, 1991, page 277.

12. Frankl, 2014, from the foreword by Harold S. Kushner, page x.

13. Riebling, M., "Personal Responsibility at the Founding," *City Journal*, Spring 2010, http://www.city-journal.org/2010/20_2_snd-personal-responsibility.html.

14. Ibid.

15. Ibid.

16. Ibid.

17. Ibid.

18. Ibid.

19. Mises, Ludwig von, 1949, pages 874–875.

Chapter 2:
Responsibility ≠ Accountability

1. The original article disappeared when the *Oz Partners Blog* was taken down and redirected to the *Partners in Leadership* website. See this blog post referencing the quote: "Accountability vs. Responsibility" The Tomorrow Lab, March 27, 2014, http://thetomorrowlab.com/2014/03/accountability-vs-responsibility/.

Chapter 3:
The Responsibility Process

1. "Create," *Dictionary.com*. Online Etymology Dictionary. Douglas Harper, historian, accessed June 3, 2016, http://dictionary.reference.com/browse/create.

Chapter 4:
The Three Keys to Responsibility

1. See http://www.dictionary.com/browse/confront, https://www.vocabulary.com/dictionary/confront.

2. "Intention," *Merriam-Webster Dictionary,* accessed June 3, 2016, http://www.merriam-webster.com/dictionary/intention.

3. "The Bucket List," Wikipedia, last modified on April 14, 2016, https://en.wikipedia.org/wiki/The_Bucket_List.

4. Nin, 1962. Origin not known (http://quoteinvestigator. com/2014/03/09/as-we-are/).

5. Weick, 1979.

6. Branden, 1999.

7. Matthew 7:4; Luke 6:42.

8. Emerson, 2015; Thoreau, 2004; Whitman, 2005.

9. Kipling, 1910.

10. Johnson, A., personal communication.

11. Attributed to Marshall Thurber by Bill McCarley during a Mastery session, January 1993.

Chapter 6:
Lead Yourself First

1. American Psychological Association, Press Release, December 14, 2000, for Jean M. Twenge, "The Age of Anxiety? Birth Cohort Change in Anxiety and Neuroticism, 1952–1993," *Journal of Personality and Social Psychology*, Vol. 749, No. 6, http://www. apa.org/news/press/releases/2000/12/anxiety.aspx.

2. Schwarzenegger, A. "Six Rules for Success," Commencement address, University of Southern California, May 15, 2009, http:// www.graduationwisdom.com/speeches/0067-schwarzenegger. htm.

3. McCarley, B. "The Characteristics of Good Goals," Co-Evolution, http://co-evolution.com/goals.php. Reprinted with permission.

4. Kimsey-House, Kimsey-House, Sandahl, & Whitworth, 2011.

5. Koch, 1999.

6. "Pareto Principle," Wikipedia, last modified April 23, 2016, https://en.wikipedia.org/wiki/Pareto_principle.

7. McKeown, 2014.

8. Sivers, 2011.

Chapter 7:
Sharing Responsibility, Sharing Leadership

1. Tichy, 2002.

2. Orazi et al., 2014.

3. Boulding, 1990.

4. Fuller, 1968.

5. Boulding, 1966. "The Economics of the Coming Spaceship Earth," ieoff.org/page160.htm.

6. George, 1879.

7. Kharas, H. & Gertz, G. Wolfensohn Center for Development at Brookings, "The New Global Middle Class: A Cross-Over from West to East," (draft version of chapter 2 in *China's Emerging Middle Class: Beyond Economic Transformation* (Cheng Li, editor), Washington, DC: Brookings Institution Press, 2010 (forthcoming), http://www.brookings.edu/~/media/research/files/papers/2010/3/china%20middle%20class%20kharas/03_china_middle_class_kharas.pdf.

8. Mackey, J. & Sisodia, R., 2013 (italics theirs).

Chapter 8:
Developing Responsibility in Others

1. Koestenbaum, P. "Personal Responsibility Paradox," *Koestenbaum's Weekly Leadership Thought*, #387, November 17, 2008, http://pib.net/index.htm.

Chapter 9:
Leading the Organization of Choice

1. Collins, 2001.

2. Thank you to Ashley Johnson for his significant contribution to codifying the five-step culture-building bridge.

Bibliography

Avery, C. M. (2001). *Teamwork Is an Individual Skill: Getting Your Work Done When Sharing Responsibility.* Berrett-Koehler.

Bandura, A. (1997). *Self-Efficacy: The Exercise of Control* (1st ed.). Worth.

Boulding, K. E. (1990). *Three Faces of Power.* Sage.

Branden, N. (1999). *The Art of Living Consciously: The Power of Awareness to Transform Everyday Life.* Touchstone.

Canfield, J., & Switzer, J. (2004). *The Success Principles: How to Get From Where You Are to Where You Want to Be.* HarperCollins.

Collins, J. (2001). *Good to Great: Why Some Companies Make the Leap . . . and Others Don't.* HarperCollins.

Covey, S. (1990). *Seven Habits of Highly Effective People* (Illustrated. ed.). Simon & Schuster.

Durant, W. (1991). *The Story of Philosophy: The Lives and Opinions of the World's Greatest Philosophers.* Pocket Books.

Emerson, R. W. (2015). *Emerson: The Ultimate Collection.* Titan Read.

Epictetus. (2014). *The Enchiridion.,* edited by Arrian, translated by Thomas Wentworth Higginson, released March 10, 2014. http://www.gutenberg.org/files/45109/45109-h/45109-h.htm.

Frankl, V. E. (2014). *Man's Search for Meaning.* (Gift ed.). Beacon Press.

Fuller, R. B. (1968). *Operating Manual for Spaceship Earth.* Simon & Schuster.

George, H. (1879). *Progress and Poverty.* http://www.henrygeorge.org/pcontents.htm.

Goldsmith, M. (2013). *What Got You Here Won't Even Get You There: How Successful People Become Even More Successful.* Profile Books.

Hill, N. (1937). *Think and Grow Rich: Teaching, for the First Time, the Famous Andrew Carnegie Formula for Money-Making, Based upon the Thirteen Proven Steps to Riches.* The Ralston Society.

Holy Bible: King James Version. (2015/2016 ed.). Christian Art Publishers.

Kimsey-House, H.; Kimsey-House, K.; Sandahl, P.; & Whitworth, L. (2011). *Co-Active Coaching: Changing Business, Transforming Lives* (3rd ed.). Nicholas Brealey America.

Kimsey-House, K.; & Kimsey-House, H. (2015). *Co-Active Leadership: Five Ways to Lead* (1st ed.). Berrett-Koehler Publishers.

Kipling, R. (1910). *Rewards and Fairies.* Charles Scribner's Sons.

Koch, R. (1999). *The 80/20 Principle: The Secret to Achieving More with Less* (Reprint ed.). Crown Business.

Mackey, J. & Sisodia, R. (2013). *Conscious Capitalism: Liberating the Heroic Spirit of Business.* Harvard Business Review Press.

Malle, B. F. (2004). *How the Mind Explains Behavior: Folk Explanations, Meaning, and Social Interaction.* MIT Press.

McKeown, G. (2014). *Essentialism: The Disciplined Pursuit of Less* (1st ed.). Crown Business.

Mises, Ludwig von. (1949). *Human Action: A Treatise on Economics*. Yale University Press.

Nin, A. (1962). *Seduction of the Minotaur* (1st ed.). Alan Swallow.

Orazi, D.; Good, L.; Robin, M.; Van Wanrooy, B.; Butar, I.; Olsen, J.; & Gahan, P. (2014, July). *Workplace Leadership: A Review of Prior Research*. Centre for Workplace Leadership. The University of Melbourne.

Peale, N. V. (1952). *The Power of Positive Thinking*. New York: Prentice-Hall.

Plato. (2009). *Five Great Dialogues of Plato: Euthyphro, Apology, Crito, Meno, Phaedo*. Coyote Canyon Press.

Robbins, T. (1992). *Awaken the Giant Within: How to Take Immediate Control of Your Mental, Emotional, Physical and Financial Destiny!* Free Press.

Schuller, R. H. (1984). *Tough Times Never Last, But Tough People Do!* (Reissue ed.). Bantam.

Sivers, D. (2011). *Anything You Want*. The Domino Project.

Thoreau, H. D. (2004). *Walden: A Fully Annotated Edition*. Yale University Press.

Tichy, N. M. (2002). *The Leadership Engine: How Winning Companies Build Leaders at Every Level*. HarperCollins.

Weick, K. E. (1979). *Social Psychology of Organizing* (Topics in Social Psychology; 2nd ed.). Addison-Wesley.

Whitman, W. (2005). *The Complete Poems* (Reprint ed.). Penguin Classics.

About the Author

Christopher Avery emphatically believes that all effective leadership starts with self. In support of that belief, he works diligently to help people activate their innate leadership ability. His groundbreaking work on The Responsibility Process has changed attitudes, careers, and cultures.

Fortune magazine called Avery's first book, *Teamwork Is an Individual Skill: Getting Your Work Done when Sharing Responsibility*, the only book on teamwork you need to read. Dr. Avery hosts The Leadership Gift™ Program, a popular eLearning system for leaders and coaches worldwide who want to master responsibility.

As CEO of the leadership development firm Partnerwerks, Inc., Christopher trains and certifies others to license and deliver The Responsibility Process content. The Leadership Excellence Awards twice recognized The Responsibility Process as a top-five leadership development tool.

Christopher has a doctorate in organizational communication from the University of Texas at Austin. He lives in Austin, Texas, with his wife Amy.

For individuals seeking convenient e-learning on the go, see
www.The.LeadershipGift.com.

For corporate services or to explore content licensing, see
www.Partnerwerks.com.

For event planners seeking a keynote speaker, see
www.ChristopherAvery.com.

Index